MANAGEMENT IN EDUCATION
— Working Papers in the Social Psychology of Educational Institutions

Contents

Introduction

During the last ten years I have been engaged in developing training programmes in education management for a wide range of teachers in all sectors of the educational system in the U.K. Much of this work has been experimental and tentative in that Education Management is a newcomer to the educational scene in the U.K. In North America Educational Administration is well developed in the school sector and so much work had been done, so much written that in what really were the pioneering days for us in the early nineteen seventies we had an enormous weight of American theory and practice to contend with. Much of the American experience was irrelevant to us but there was a whole mass of "theory" that could not be replaced until we had enough theory of our own.

Latterly there have developed social psychological approaches to Educational Administration in North America but the interpretations appear to be highly influenced by American culture while the dead weight of academic respectability of the wrong kind has prevented American theoriests from going forward as forcefully as they might have done. Recent controvercies over the "theory" movement and the emergence of phenomenology have made little difference. The Americans still seem to hold a hard party line on a certain sociological theory, and the existentialism and phenomology that appeals much more to the European mind and experience does not attract Americans so much.

My own theory has developed over the years and hopefully is still in process of change and vigorous evaluation. I have been greatly influenced by the humanistic stream of social psychology though I would call myself a psycho-sociologist because I am interested in individuals first and organisations only secondly. The collected papers reflect that view and its development. They were all written for some specific occasion—consultancy, a seminar, a class and are in many ways incomplete. But the all are an attempt to apply theory to practice rather than just develop a theory. In a later volume, I intend to develop more coherently concepts in education management but the present collection is intended to open debate and controversy and to encourage practitioners to consider their present practice and perhaps change it.

The book is not intended to be read from cover to cover, but to be dipped into where the chapter titles create interest. Because these are essentially working papers, they have an element of repetition which I have left so that each idea can stand on its own in its own context.

H. L. GRAY
Netherthong
November, 1979.

1.
Management Theory and Education

There are many misconceptions about management. It is often thought that management is a precise technique or collection of techniques that can be applied to almost any situation with the consequence of immediate improvement. But the word 'management' is no more exact than the word 'organise' or even the word 'teach', though, it is a generally useful word to describe the activities necessary to influence, control, direct or influence people who have come together with a common purpose. While it is true that there is a great deal written and spoken about management 'techniques', techniques are aids to management not the whole of management itself. It is certainly a delusion to believe that one can be taught techniques that will ensure immediate (or even eventual) effectiveness in situations that require management. Indeed, one of the great disservices of 'management education' has been the formulation of the idea that there is an exact science of management that can be learned like engineering or botany or computer programming. An even more unfortunate development has been a rise in expectations that management 'techniques' from one area can be applied in essentially the same way to other situations. The idea of 'education management' often suffers from this misconception so it is important for us to try to understand what exactly (or, more correctly, inexactly) management means in the context of education.

Management 'theory' is rationalisation about management activity. That is to say, a manager or management 'thinker' reflects on his experience and attempts to make sense of it. He interprets what he has seen or experienced and attempts to make valid generalisations from it. In making generalisations or hypotheses he begins to develop a theory of management. If he interprets his experience of management as strong, firm leadership, then he will derive a theory of strong, firm leadership as a key concept in his idea of management. Most management ideas are pragmatic in this sense and are interpretations of experience. Other managers have different experiences and express their theories differently. Most management theory is subjective because it focusses on the practicalities of bosses getting other people to work for them and develops around personal preferences in behaviour. My own view of management theory is not intended to be cynical but rather to be realistic. Managers tend to need answers quickly and to live lives characterised by considerable urgency. They make decisions intuitively and forthrightly because they are usually under great pressure from a wide range of other people. We are still in an age when managers like to listen to other managers tell how they do things and they often justify what they do by the 'results', almost always quantifiable matters.

Management is a comparatively recent concept, just about one

9

hundred years old*. It has invariably been associated with commercial necessity and financial investment, and only since the second world war has the idea of 'management' been extended to other areas of human activity and organisation. There is still a considerable confusion about management as a commercial tool and management as a concept of organisation. Yet we should more properly apply ourselves to the understanding of organisation, because management is an aspect of organisation. Techniques of management tend to be technical instruments and procedures (increasingly computerised systems) but the use of techniques depends on an understanding of the nature of organisation. Increasingly the understanding of management is coming to depend on an understanding of how people behave in organisations. Techniques fall into place when we understand how they relate to people but the understanding of people must be the first concern. Banks and railways could be entirely automated but management would still have to concern itself with the people who use banks and railways; the technologists could do what they like to the systems but without being concerned with people, they would not be managers. Managers, then, are people who deal with people in organisations and we must understand how organisations function if we are to understand management.

In education, there is very little technology but a good deal of human organisation. In essence, education is a relationship between a teacher and a learner (or between two learners). Learning can be mechanised in various ways but by and large education is generally recognised as an interpersonal activity. One runs schools with people not machines. However many mechanical aids to learning there may be, people are always paramount so if we talk of management in education, we are almost entirely concerned with people. In this respect, education is a good model for management because since it has only a peripheral commercial purpose it presents us very clearly with problems of interpersonal relationships or human organisation that are obscured in so many other cases.

The basis for a theory of management should properly be a theory of organisation. Doubtless organisation theory is no less subjective than a theory of management but it is of a different order. If management theory is in all likelihood an expression of personal preference about how managers ought to behave, organisation theory is a reflecting on how people are perceived to behave. So organisation theory is an aspect

---

* F. W. Taylor read a paper entitled "A piece rate system" to the American Society of Mechanical Engineers in 1895; this is generally considered to be the beginning of the idea of management as a distinct concept.

of social psychology – the behaviour of people in organisations. Organisation theory is descriptive of how people behave collectively and predictive of how they are likely to behave when formally organised. Formal organisation is simply a pattern of behaviour constant over a period of time and repeated in some way. A bus queue, by this defintion, would be formal behaviour but it would not become organisational until someone began to influence the behaviour of the people in the queue. Once influence is exerted on or within a group, formal organisation occurs in predictable patterns – or at least in patterns which could have been predicted though they seldom are entirely predictable in practice.

Management theory tends to assume a greater degree of prediction than actually occurs. Since management is about control, the best theory will lead to greatest prediction and most control. At a low level (e.g. the behaviour of students in a college assembly) prediction is often accurate but in critical situations, prediction is a matter of open choice. Organisation theory is less concerned with prediction than exploration though as a consequence its predictions are greater. Organisation theory is not concerned only with overt and superficial behaviour but also with psychological reasons and motives. Perhaps at this point the destinction between management theory and organisation theory becomes blurred but it is important only to realise that what concerns us is the reality of organisational behaviour rather than the deception about what goes on when people organise themselves.

While organisations are 'objective' in that certain key characteristics can be generally agreed – location, size, numbers of people concerned – the ways in which we understand them are quite subjective. This is one of the basic problems of organisation theory*. However much we may be able to describe objectively an organisation, each of the members will perceive what is going on quite subjectively. It is because of the multiplicity of subjective perceptions of the organisation that 'management' is such a problematical but exciting activity. We must use certain terms to describe an organisation and there has grown up an important vocabulary of organisation theory, but once we have learned to use the terms, we have to subject them to scrutiny to discover the meaning of the organisation to each member for whom a given issue is critical.

All organisations have structure but 'structure' is only a description of what happens in the organisation; it is not a separate entity so there cannot be imposed a structure on an organisation. We can, however, bring about changes in behaviour and as behaviour becomes character-

---

* From now on we shall use the term 'organisation theory' instead of 'management theory' unless a distinction has to be made.

istically patterned we observe characterstic structure. Labels on people in an organisation tell us very little about how they behave, though they may tell us how they are 'expected' to behave. Understanding the nature of organisational structure is often the biggest problem for newcomers to organsation theory because they cannot understand how structure can be so fluid. Yet the essential characteristic of organisation is fluidity or its 'organic' quality. Just how fuid an organisation is depends on how control is exerted and the amount of freedom members feel themselves able to exercise. There is always more freedom of structure in an organisation than members ever realise and the work of consultants is frequently with increasing the amount of permitted movement in the organisation.

The drawing up of organisation charts is more often than not a method of control than a description of real relationships. In the same way, job descriptions are more often prescriptive than liberating. Good management should be concerned with freeing up the personal energy in an organisation since the more energy available the more the organisation can grow and develop but often managers want to limit freedom for economic as well as personal reasons. For educational institutions there is a real issue between whether more freedom can be given or more control and direction imposed. On the whole, educational institutions do not encourage a great deal of creativity but are more concerned to regulate closely the behaviour of the members towards certain clear but limited goals—examinations.

Though we may think of organisations as impersonal entities – the word 'institution' implies this – they are in fact 'collectives'. That is, they consist of people engaged in collective activity. This being so, organisations can hardly be said to have goals though their members may do so. It is better, therefore, to think of organisations as serving purposes for the members and for goals to be objectives which individuals agree to pursue for personal and individual ends, or to gratify certain personal needs. It is important to understand that the only goals are personal ones and that no one's personal needs can arbitarily override anothers. Sometimes, bosses or other individuals objectify their personal needs into organisational needs and, perhaps more often, personalise organisational needs so that organisational and personal needs are seen to coincide. But a boss cannot say that his personal needs and those of the organisation are identical without exerting excessive influence over his colleagues. The exercise of authority within organisations is a major critical aspect of organisational dynamics for it is always difficult to determine just how legitimate the exercise of authority by any individual or group may be over others. Managers are inclined to assume that they have greater authority than they in fact

12

have. That they always have less than they believe is evidenced by the crises faced by organisations when decisions are not fully implemented.

The dynamics of organisations can best be understood by observing the dynamics of small groups. There is an extensive literature on group dynamics which has produced a valuable vocabulary. Already we have used the terms structure, membership and authority; others will be introduced as we proceed. Organisations are very difficult and subtle phenomena to understand. It is impossible to understand everything that is happening in a large organisation like a school or college by simply observing; the essential dynamics are beyond observation. But we can use our experience of small groups to create personal models of organisation and from these we can extrapolate to larger institutions*. These organisation models are psycho-sociological in that they derive from an understanding of the psychological relationships between group members and the way issues and problems in the group are realised and dealt with. The dynamics of a group and organisation are the processes by which the various tasks of the group are accomplished. It is customary to speak of 'process' as the description of how groups behave and 'task' or 'content' as what these groups attempt to achieve. Since dynamics are by definition fluid and changing any description of an organisation can be no more than a snap-shot picture of what was going on; changes between the moment of analysis and the present may be very considerable indeed.

Change is characteristic of organisations; that is to say, it is in the nature of organisations for them to be constantly changing. Though people may try to impose specific kinds of change on an organisation, or seek to bring about certain changes within an organisation, change is a constant reality and there is no means of knowing what is or is not a 'natural' change. On the other hand, it does seem likely that there are certain changes that are 'more natural than others' — that is, changes that would occur if there were no conscious or deliberate efforts to bring about change. One of these natural tendencies is towards break up since all organisations break up eventually. Another change is away from one kind of order towards another. Since all conscious management effort is aimed at order and the continuance of the organisation (or its replacement), organisations will experience the tension between break up and order. It seems probable that many organisations are kept in existence long after they have ceased to serve their most useful purposes.

---

* I have explained how we may do this in my later paper "Training People to Understand Organisations" A Clinical Approach.

13

Utility is another important idea in organisation theory. If people engage in purposeful activity — and for the most part this is what they seem to do — then organisations have continually to serve useful purposes. Thus usefulness will be variously and subjectively judged but it can be assumed that members require consciously or unconsciously to get something out of their membership. That 'No one is in it for nothing' is a useful maxim if we are to fully understand organisational behaviour. Each individual is in the organisation in expectation of a 'return' for his membership — for some form of social and pyschological exchange. In organsational terms there is no such thing as pure altruism; altruism is simply a mutual self interest. To look at organisational membership in this way is itself useful and enlightening for it enables us to explain a good deal that is puzzling about why people join, and especially remain in, an organisation. So far as educational institutions are concerned this is a useful way of understanding the teaching/learning relationship and of uncovering the kinds of satisfactions that membership gives.

It is axiomatic that no two individuals perceive an organisation in precisely the same way. We view everything in the light of our experience. That means we perceive the reality in organisations differently and interpret events accordingly. We all have experience of 'good' and 'bad' days which do not coincide with other people's 'good' and 'bad' days so that one is jaundiced while another is euphoric and vice versa. One way of understanding these different perceptions is to view them as fantasies. We each have our fantasies about an organisation to which we belong and interpret what we see and experience in terms of our fantasies. Where the fantasies of different people are compatible or congruent no problems arise, but where they are incompatible considerable difficulties can ensue*. Irreconcilable differences between people arise because they cannot understand the nature of one another's fantasies, indeed are often totally unaware of them. This theory partly explains differences that disorientate people by finding the atmosphere of an organisation just simply uncongenial, unsypathetic or discomfiting.

Each organisation develops its own culture or ethos. That is to say there is a prevalent system of values, customs and mores which are peculiar to and characteristic of that organisation. In schools, terms such as 'ethos' or 'tone' may be used and they refer to what is generally thought to be indefinable but characteristic. In reality, it is much less undefinable than inmates often assume because it is possible to discover dominant values and behaviours by careful observation and

---

* I have devloped this idea in "Organisations as Subjectivities".

discussion. The 'feel' or 'ambience' of a place is essentially a consequence of behaviour patterns which in turn derive from personal attitudes and values. These become manifest in quite tangible matters, events, procedures and behaviours which are so taken for granted by members that they fail to see them and recognise their significance.

There are, of course, a lot of matters not obvious to the onlooker, but an experienced and perceptive onlooker can see a long way behind the superficialities. Human intuition is much more active than many are ready to concede. Much of our training and education is to detach ourselves from natural sensitivities yet we can only ever come to understand organisations when our natural senses have been re-educated.

Understanding organisations is not a magical or esoteric skill. It is a necessity for all of us because we spend most of our life in organsations of one sort or another. Membership demands survival but more than that an awareness of ourself as a member is vital if the usefulness rather than the destructiveness of organisations is to be experienced by us. All too many organisations are places of missed opportunities, lost battles, frustrating experiences, pious and unrealistic hopes. With understanding they can be a means of personal enrichment.

The dichotomy in management is always between the interests and needs of the individual against those of the organisation, though in practice this means the needs of one individual against the needs of another. As we have seen, there is no such thing as an objective organisation only one that is identified in various ways with various people. Depersonalising organisations is the great fallacy of management theory and one of the destructive errors of organisation thinking. Always in organisations the interests of one individual are being brought against the interest of another and the conflict is furthered by colluding into group issues ('management' versus 'workers'). Since all relationships involve some form of bargaining and all bargaining is a form of conflict, it follows that organisations are arenas of conflict. We might even say that conflict is the latent dynamics of organisations. As we resolve conflict, so organisational activity takes place. When it is resolved in the best interest of all those involved, the organisation is healthy; when the resolution is one sided there is trouble. Few organisations have mechanisms for the satisfactory resolution of conflict and so trouble arises*. Much management thinking aims to avoid conflict and that is a major error. Conflict avoidance and consequent flight from the real issues puts an organisation into a state of

---

* See my paper "Exchange and Conflict in the School". in Houghton, V, et al Management in Education, Ward Lock/OU 1976.

psychological suspension. The real work (conflict resolution) cannot go on and anxiety and frustration ensue. Conflict resolution must be mutually acceptable if it is to be fruitful to the organisation and so solutions that are the result of managerial coercion are dysfunctional.

Organisations are replete with rewards and punishments, part of the psychological exchange that must go on. When rewarding and punishing is arrogated to a manager the potential for unresolved conflict increases. Provided a manager is perceived to be a genuine 'third party' in conflict resolution, he can serve a useful purpose as arbiter, facilitator or umpire but where (as is usually the case) he is seen as arbiter by authority of his position rather than his personal position as a member, then problems of great seriousness arise for he exercises personal judgements and preferences in line with his own selfish needs and increases his coercive power over other members. That this is what happens in organisations is the greatest pity; a consequence of our social attitudes towards power, control and authority but in terms of pure organisation theory no one can take unto himself, or be given by an outside agent, power over members that does not derive from his relationships with those members, without dire consequences. It is these dire consequences that are at the root of many organisational (and hence management) problems that we have to deal with day by day.

Within the organisation, each person has a position, or rather a number of positions, in which he relates to other members. In organisational terms these positions are called 'roles', a role being the behaviours associated with a position in terms of the interactions among people in the organisation. Every member of an organisation by virtue of his membership has a position, and role behaviour develops as a simple consequence of the passage of time. Usually titles or names (e.g. manager, secretary) are given to roles in the expectation that the role 'incumbant' will follow a traditional pattern of behaviour generally associated with that role. But the functions of his role do not belong to the title but to the organisation. It is no use calling a leader of a climbing party a secretary and expecting him to type letters instead of leading a climb, and this is true of all roles; roles are determined by organisational needs not by designations. Around roles are expectations, the way other members expect roles to be worked out and fulfilled. None of the expectations exactly coincide so there will always be discrepancies between expectation and fulfilment as well as different expectations. When the differences are significant, there arise critical issues for the 'organisation'. Most people fall back on what they believe ought to be appropriate role behaviour without trying to find out what has happened, why it has happened and how it may better fit into the reality of organisational behaviour rather than hypothetical expectation.

Behaviour in organisations occurs for the most part in groups or in relation to groups. Organisations may be considered a federation or coalition of groups. It has been suggested that educational institutions like universities are loosely bound groups while schools consist of tightly bound groups. Sometimes the importance of groups overshadows the importance of individuals yet individuals come before groups. Each individual enters an organisation as a person in his own right with a whole idiosyncratic range of needs and talents, a distinct personality. Mangers often forget the importance of individuality perhaps because it is easier to deal with objects rather than real flesh and blood people. Personality, too, as a concept is very difficult to handle because there are so many approaches to understanding (and describing) personality. We can however be clear about two things. Each individual will behave fairly consistently and true to type (that is, his own character/personality type) and he will be somewhere (again fairly predictably) between being an authoritarian and/or dependent person and being collaborative and/or autonomous. By and large we can be fairly certain that however we interpret an individual, his behaviour will be consistent in personality terms and in terms of organisational behaviour. If this were not so, interpersonal relations would be virtually impossible. It is these two truths about individuals that make organisation analysis possible.

A useful theory of personality and organisation that blends an explanation of personality theory and organisation theory derives from a scheme proposed by O. J. Harvey*. It suggests four stages of personal development and four stages of group or organisation development. These stages are dependence, counter dependence, interdependence and independence. The usefulness of this idea – which sounds naive as related here in bald terms – is that it suggests how personality and organisational culture or climate match or mismatch. An individual who is psychologically dependent will feel most at home in an organisation that creates dependency by having strong autocratic or paternalistic leaders, likewise with other phases. The important idea arising from the theory is that when we look at people in organisations we should always be looking for matches and mismatches between individuals and organisational climate. We can do this with whatever theory of personality we may prefer, for example the Jungian theory of types or Personal Construct theory. Detailed analysis can only be made by a careful study of people as persons and organisations as cultures.

---

* *Harvey O. J., Hunt David E. & Schroder H. M. Conceptual Systems & Personality Organisation, John Wiley NY 1961.*

17

Organisations do not remain static, in the same state. The inherent tendency to change has already been mentioned but there are phases of development that are important to our understanding. Organisations have a starting up phase during which new members are recruited and certain routines and practices are laid down. This is followed by a consolidation phase in which there may or may not be a significant change in membership. After this comes a period of stability and then some form of expansion or renewal. Periods of quiescence and activity alternate from then onwards until the organisation closes down. These phases can be predicted only with the grossest generalisation but what does appear incontrovertible is that oranisations do pass through phases of development and that these phases require different kinds of responses from members. The kind of boss who is happy in a period of expansion and novelty will quite probably be unhappy during a period of consolidation. Similarly, a member who functions well during a period that requires much routine work will be unhappy when he is required to change his style towards entrepreneurship so that the organisation can grow. It may well be that leaders should be changed for various phases and some mechanisms will have to be devised to assist them to take on different roles.

Related to the development of organisations, in the sense of their changing nature, is the concept of career. Organisations are locations during the career of an individual. It is not possible to pursue a career without being involved with organisations, at least at essential points. An individual will usually be a member of several schools or colleges during his professional career as a teacher. He will look on each institution as a place where his current career needs can be fulfilled and these needs will change from institution to institution. There is another example of the need to match individuals and organisations. Organisation needs arise from the needs of the people in the organisation; they require help and assistance from someone else whom they seek to recruit. An individual looking for a new job may be very conscious of the need for promotion (a form of recognition) but he will be dissatisfied with promotion alone. Status may not be enough, certainly not for a long period of time. What he will be looking for are opportunities to use his skills and talents and to feel a part of the organisation; that is, one of a group of people with congruent interests and work styles. There can be nothing impersonal about an organisation; often the quality of material surroundings has low significance measured against a feeling of happiness or contentment. Recruitment is an essential part of organisational functioning and members need to be exceedingly careful about how it is done. The idea of career is often interpreted as promotion but that can only be a part of the story since not everyone can reach the top. If not being 'promoted' is seen as a condemnation or punishment then we are in a highly judgemental situation. Organisations cannot function with everyone at the top and it would appear unquestionable that all members are of some kind of "equal" importance. The belief that only the people at the top are important hardly bears examination yet it is one of those myths that it is difficult to discount. Careers are about finding places where an individual can find most personal fulfilment and this may or may not involve adultation by others. The mistake so often made by mid-range members is to denigrate the importance of their junior colleagues. Perhaps it is significant that it is impossible to find language to describe locations in an organisation that is not hierarchical and often judgemental. The problems of hierarchy in organisations are ones that we shall return to time and again because status seems to be a preoccupation with members of our society at large.

It is comparatively easy to outline the vocabulary of organisation theory and it is not very difficult to understand because most of the words and phrases come from ordinary speech even if the social psychologist does make something of a jargon of them. Applying the terms to specific organisations is a little more difficult because our experience of any organisation is so overlaid with our whole social experience. Even until quite recently many teachers rejected the whole idea of management applied to education as being totally outside their experience of what was needed in education. As interest in education management grew it resulted in an attempt to foist industrial and commercial techniques onto education — usually with little understanding of either industry or education. More recently interest in organisation theory rather than management "theory" has grown up as has been indicated in the earlier part of this chapter. So the best way of understanding an organisation is simply in terms of our experience of it rather than in terms of how we think an organisation should be organised. Obviously our experience of a small primary school is different from that of a large polytechnic.

An issue that has preoccupied many people is that of the size of the institution. It is held that the most critical factor in differentiating among organisations is the factor of size. That is, significant features are a function of (derive directly from) the size of the organisation. This is only partly true because size is not itself a uniform matter. A polytechnic with 7,000 students on a single campus is different from a polytechnic with 7,000 students on ten campuses. Only some management functions have universal applicability throughout the institution. Furthermore, is a primary school of 200 children a single institution or is it one campus of primary education in a Local Education Authority of seven thousand primary school children? Here is the key to understanding organisations. Whatever the size of the organisation, activity will occur effectively in smaller units and these units will be social units of five or six people. Of course, administrative demands may be on a larger scale and the effect of bureaucratic procedures will be to enforce delays, but it does not seem to follow that overall large units are more effective or efficient than small units *per se* and the reverse is equally true. Although there is a suggestion that very large units are inefficient (certainly they may be impersonal) it has yet to be satisfactorily demonstrated firstly that large institutions are either better or worse than small ones and secondly, that small institutions have any advantage over large ones. Because an individual has a certain kind of experience of a certain type of organisation it does not follow that everyone else will have the same experience. While it is the individual experience that is important, we must be careful not to extrapolate to a broad generalisation from one experience. Education is bedevilled by complete lack of research into the effects of size but there are many untested assumptions. Every educational institution will have membership, location, times of working and will be embedded in a socio-economic environment. It will provide a distinctive experience for everyone who comes into membership, however brief that period of membership may be, and in describing that experience we describe something of the culture of the institution, an experience of the ethos. It is probably more important, pragmatically, to understand how one comes to experience an institution in a certain way than to be able to analysise statistically what goes to make up an institution (number on roll, staff/student ratio; types of rooms and educational materials provided etc). Most analyses with which we will be familiar are of the quantitative, statistical type and they tell us very little unless we want to make financial decisions (though perhaps, in the end, all decisions are financial ones!). We need to know more than that the size of the English Department is 10 teachers, four of whom are part-time and six women with a head of department who is aged 38. We soon become interested in the personalities of the people in the department and how they interact. We become interested in the role of the married women and how their careers develop around their growing children. We note that the Head of Department is keen on promotion to a Headship and is trying to gain favour to be promoted to second deputy of the school. We discover that three of the departments want to teach drama and communication skills while two continually regret the days of formal grammar. These kinds of behaviour and relationships are what organisation theory is all about. They explain motivation, commitment, ambition, leadership style, alienation, disgruntlement and so on—all the behaviours that are the subject matter of social psychology. To describe educational institutions in these terms is to make an analysis of use to the task of managing the organisation.

The task of management is to facilitate the development of the organisation. Earlier management was described somewhat pejoratively as control. That is true but control may be authoritarian and judgemental or facilitative and accepting. Managers are required to make decisions by virtue of their positions but how they make those decisions is a matter for their choice. Because organisations exist only for the people who are their members—that is, in practice organisations can perform only what their members are willing and able to perform—it is important for members to have a genuine feeling of being part of the organisation, or rather as much a part as they feel the need to be. The job of the manager is to mediate among the various demands made and the various kinds of commitment members and clients will give. He does this in situations such as that of the English Department described above. Each distinct group of members has a distinct range of demands, commitments and contributions.

In education—as in hospitals and other service organisations—there are two groups of membership. All organisations have members and clients or customers but in education there are at least two groups of members and at least two groups of customer. The members are teachers and students who have different career needs in the school. The customers, or clients, are the parents of pupils and the 'consumer' or employer of the pupils when they leave. It is better to think of employers as part of the general environment in which the school must function as a socio-economic entity. Employers as a group are no more unified or real than society at large and in some ways too much credence is given to what some employers say at a given time. Employment prospects are much wider than many employees are able to envisage. Parents, however, do have a special relationship to the school since the task of education that the school performs is on behalf of the parents. The student however is neither customer nor even client. He is a full member of the school although there is some differentiation of function. Exactly how this function is perceived will depend on the philosophy of education of the perceiver. If we see learning as a partnership we shall have one view of educational organisation (structure) different from those who see teaching as a didactic relationship. Perhaps increasingly teaching is coming to be seen as a two way relationship and this is certainly so in Higher and Further Education. Hence the organisation of teaching will depend on the philosophy of education of the heads and teachers; it will be an expression of their understanding of the educational relationship.

However large the educational institution, the primary task will

21

always – by definition – be teaching (or the creation of teaching/learning situations). Management has no other purpose than to facilitate this activity. Since no human activity is organisationally simpler than that between a teacher and his student, the more complex educational organisations become, the less likely they are to fulfil their function.

2.
How Can We Understand Organisations?

The development of theories about organisations in the last 60 to 70 years shows a distinct move from a view that organisations are inherently impersonal structures towards the view that organisations are essentially collections of people with individual needs and contributions. Organisation theories almost always derive from problems of management and are more properly called management theories since they concern themselves with how organisations can be better 'organised' or managed. The impetus for researching about organisations has arisen from the need to solve management problems concerning matters such as rewards, motivation, control and leadership. In order to gain general acceptability, organisation theories are made to pass the test of being apparently practical—the term indicates a way to better practice. While it is by no means unreasonable to expect theories to have application, the changes in theory lead one to wonder if there have ever been any truly fundamental theories of management/organisation or only abstract solutions to problems as currently perceived in accordance with the contemporary cultural values.

The defining quality of a theory is that it provides an internally coherent way of looking at phenomena in a described field so that the generalisations of the theory can be applied in specific cases. The terms of the application are consistent, inherent in the theory and special to the specific instance. Yet all *management* theory generalises from the particular to the general; nearly all *organisation* theory generalises from hypothetical solutions to management problems. These statements appear to be true of, for example, Weber's theory of bureaucracy, the administrative theory of Chester Barnard, the Sociol-Technical theory of Trist and the Tavistock and Norwegian schools, and the pragmatism of all business managers.

What are the problems for developing a theory?

There seems little doubt of the need to develop some basic theory of organisations; a base or ground upon which an understanding of organisations can be developed and which will give some unity and integrity to what people write about organisations. There have been only a few attempts to provide basic concepts to thinking about organisations perhaps the most important of which has been general systems theory. The advantage of general systems theory is that it applies to other areas of investigation than formal human organisation and provides a supposedly value-free framework for investigation. However, the social-scientists concerned with looking at organisations and using general systems theory have in every case jumped from a value-free framework of organisations as open systems to a value-laden

25

interpretation of the nature of human (organisation) systems. For the systems concept to be valid for examining human organisation we should need to know what actually are the systems and subsystems that exist and this would require an analysis not unlike that required for the identification of species of plants. As it is, systems theories of organisation always *assume* the reality of the systems and subsystems described and pre-determined the descriptive categories such as leadership, product, control, and so on, or local, regional and national systems.

At its crudest, the systems model of the school takes a graphic view of the school as the central subsystem of concentric circles of larger environmental meta-systems. Even the term 'environment' is used in a contentious manner which assumes that organisational environments are external to one another even though they act upon them. Of course, a simplistic systems model may well be useful for ordering the chapters in a book or sorting out priorities in a research project but the open systems concept of input, throughput and output are not even adequately descriptive of the sausage making process (because so many essential things occur that are not directly a part of that 'process') let alone human membership of organisations. The use to which the general systems theory of organisations has been put has invariably involved changing the organisation towards a desired direction by assuming that there is a particular, reasonably clear primary task* and this task almost always turns out to be related to the organisation *qua* organisation rather than the members as people. In all the systems descriptions, there is an assumption that the organisation has preeminence over the membership though with the tendency for personal identification with the organisational task to increase up the managerial hierarchy to the boss – where interests are perceived as identical with those of the organisation. Although systems theory points out that all organisations are part of other organisations and hence are dependent on them in some way, the influence of the external environment is generally considered to be more *important* than the needs of the sub-organisation. In short, users of general systems theories of organisations soon interpose values and the question arises as to whether systems theories of organisations have any basic categories of analysis that are essentially neutral in significance.

The extention of the question is, is there a theory of organisations that is, or can be, essentially value free and if not, are there alternatives? The problem is one of observation, description and analysis. Can human

---

* e.g. E. J. Miller & A. K. Rice: Systems of Organisation, Tavistock London 1967.

behaviour be observed in any way that is not biased so that even if categories could be devised for description, could bias or interpretation be avoided? At the present time it seems unlikely that there is any possibility of making objective observations of human behaviour: even the choice of categories is subjective and selective, the observer being too much a part of the culture he observes. Human behaviour is always complex with several motives and reasons present at any time. A simple example is the 'observation' that two people are crossing the road—the significance of the act and awareness will be quite different for each of them. For a blind person a highly charged and dangerous situation; for a teenage lad intent on meeting his girlfriend hardly any awareness of crossing a busy street. However apparently similar the acts may be, their significance is different; any truly scientific observation would be concerned with such significance.

If we use the kind of categories that are currently used in organisation theory (especially the sociological and psychological) we have not only categories that can only be useful if they are "properly" interpreted but categories the significance and definition of which have not been adequately determined. For instance, we use terms like "motivation" and "leadership" as aspects of organisational behaviour but motivation is something that can only exist within the person motivated while leadership relates to behaviour of a number of individuals. There has been no attempt to define and relate the terminology used in talking about organisations to proper scientific categories. The social sciences abound in semantic difficulties, and, of course, it is more than likely that such scientific precision is not appropriate. For example, the social sciences tend to use mathematical and statistical formulae in an idiosyncratic way. Mathematical relationships are deemed to indicate relationships between phenomena in a way that is often logically improper. Observations are assumed to be accurate when, as has been illustrated above, the 'observations' are little more than speculative deductions. The need for the social sciences to demonstrate their credibility by using the formulae from true sciences is by now pathological. Literary criticism, religious studies, law, language studies, history find no need to quantify so relentlessly and appear none the worse and to be held in no less esteem. (In fact, it is remarkable how many competent natural scientists are highly religious men when not a single item of religious faith will stand up either to scientific scrutiny or even logical argument.) It seems almost ridiculous that organisation theory which is demonstrably pragmatic in the event and has so clearly failed to be either scientific or logical should persist in its image as a pseudo-science. Clearly we need to look in some other direction for credibility and validity.

Things are what they seem

The one fact about organisation that is self-evident is that everyone sees his organisation in a different way from everyone else. Teachers and pupils view schools differently from one another as members of categories and also as individuals. In fact, in terms of their view of the school, "teacher" and "pupil" are unlikely to be valid categories indicating discrete differences except on specified dimensions. A head may view things differently from his subordinates; his subordinates may not even perceive themselves as subordinates. (And this gives the lie to the validity of some of the categories as used in general systems theories of organisations.) We may, of course, try to redefine categories and redefine our definitions but the more we do this, the less manageable the information. Redefining species and subspecies of plants is a different matter since we are dealing with permanent differences; with human beings as members of organisations there are no inherent and permanent differences. To try to look at organisations from outside appears to be a hopeless and useless task. But it is equally difficult to try to gather information from within the organisation, since in doing this the investigator often does not make hypotheses which he tests, he makes assumptions which he seeks to confirm. For example, let us take the idea of organisational climate. It seems quite logical to assume that organisations have emotional or psychological climates — after all, families do; some are 'friendly', others are 'tense'. But then these terms are statements of my response to the situation, not necessarily that of the members. They are subjective interpretations. All right, so what if we ask the members what they feel about the organisation (and we take for granted not only that they are willing to express their feelings, but even that they know what their feelings are) can we still say that the climate of the organisation is 'friendly'! Only if everyone not only says just that, but also means the same thing by it. However, what do we do with this data when we have collected it? Will it still be valid and for how long? Is 'friendliness' a characteristic of the climate or a response to other things that occur — such as having a lot of personal friends as colleagues, even if one hates the boss (who may never be present any way)? Furthermore, in collecting data about climate, the researcher will almost certainly have decided which climates he approves of and of which he disapproves. The fact that a climate may be neither generally friendly nor unfriendly just isn't in his book of rules.

What can be known?

Can we, then, know nothing? Is there no reality? It looks rather as if the only reality is the perceived reality of the individual, whoever he is.

28

What is real for me may not be real for anyone else — and reality is what I believe to be real, that to which I react. This is an existentialist view with which the reader must be already familiar but the question is most serious — if there are no ways of understanding organisations *objectively*, are there any ways of understanding them *subjectively?* If every individual makes his own interpretation of reality and that is valid for him, how can we understand these differences and discover if they have significance when the individuals are both parts of the 'same' organisation? It seems almost certain that there is a need to understand organisations if only because their very existence requires responding and coping behaviour. Maybe, for instance, managerial behaviour is not control behaviour at all, but rather coping behaviour; the way in which an individual copes with his position in the organisation. In other words, organisational behaviour is the way in which we cope with the world with which others present us. Our perception of the organisation is the framework and conceptual basis which forms the rationale for our behaviour. That is, in order to know what to do we have to define our world and situation in fairly simple and selective terms in order to limit the ways we respond to ways with which we feel fairly comfortable. For instance, I am deferential towards my boss because that is the way which is most comfortable to me. Infact, he may prefer me to be aggressive but because I cannot risk trying out alternatives I choose the one with which I feel most safe.

In this view, organisations (formal and informal) can only be explained in terms of the understanding and perceptions of those who are members and those who are observers.* If this brings organisation theory near to any other academic field, it must be the general area of psychology-psychiatry; near to psycho-analysis and psycho-therapy. Both these fields have their problems of scientific credibility but no more so than medicine where definition of illness, disease and health are also problematic not to mention the appropriateness of 'cures' for 'illness'. But at least medicine and psychiatric medicine work as the matching of what the patient believes and what understanding the practitioner is intelligent enough to bring to the situation. A physician who assumes that most complaints are influenza will not always be right; he must have other possibilities in mind including the possibility of the unique syndrome (since no two people suffer from the same disease in quite the same way; as, for instance, in the case of multiple or disseminated sclerosis, the naming of which is not even satisfactory).

---

* Since many organisations, especially public organisations, have significance for many people who are not organisational members e.g. tax departments, the post office, schools, police departments and so on.

The advantages of moving away from technical kinds of descriptions of organisations to medical/psyciatric ones lies in the significance of the metaphors we use — since all descriptions of organisations are metaphorical — but also in the openess and caution of the approach. In psychiatry, the practitioner is forced into trying to understand what the patient says; he is also concerned not to categorise the condition any more than necessary. It is, for instance, notoriously difficult to get a psychiatrist to define a person as in need of mental certification, but organisation/management consultants readily assume they can put the organisation to rights. Indeed, the current mood in management thinking is that all organisations can be improved in some way or another. While it may be true that all organisations can be *changed,* the desirability of that change must remain a matter of opinion since even on a systems theory basis the long term and ultimate effects of that change cannot be known for some considerable time, if at all.

A phenomenological approach

Intrinsic to the psychiatric, medical, psycho-therapeutic approaches to observation and deduction is what has come to be termed a phenomenological stance. Since 'phenomenological' looks like being a revived term in management theory and due for over-exposure in the next decade, and since agreement on definition is not yet resolved, we can state here what a phenomenological approach to the study of organisation would mean. At least such a definition made now will enable discussion to centre on the validity of subsequent argument here and will not divert to general semantic debate in another area of concern. The phenomenological view of organisations assumes that each individual makes his own sense of, and gives his own meaning to, the organisations to which he belongs. Whether an organisation is 'formal' or 'informal' will be a matter of his own interpretation though formal and informal can be taken to be limits in a continuum from high ritual and prescription to low ritual and little prescription. Of course, no-ritual and no-prescription of behaviour would not be organisation. We can define organisation as any situation of human interaction in which patterns of behaviour can be observed. I know of no other definition that is entirely satisfactory.

To understand an organisation from a phenomenological point of view one needs to know what people think about that organisation. Clearly we can never know what *everyone* thinks about it — nor do we ever need to know. If a problem is diagnosed the person who is most significant is the one who defines the problem. Thus, for a manager to say "My workers are lazy," is for him to say "To me, my workers are lazy," and we can only understand the problem of laziness if we understand why the manager believes them to be so. 'Laziness' is *his* problem, not the workers. The issue here is how I can understand why laziness is a problem to the manager. It is the problem of understanding and interpretation to which we have already referred when discussing research design. Polling workers about their attitude will be of little help since the only question we can ask is, "Do you think you are lazy?" and the answer is likely to be "No." To find out if they are lazy we need production statistics but even then we would be assuming that production figures and laziness correlate. Obviously we need a different kind of probing and to do this we need some sort of a hypothesis — but since the situation cannot be a technical one, we cannot use a scientific instrument. We would be better advised to examine how, why and when we make the hypothesis — in other words, to ask why we have such a hunch, to examine our intuition. Most usefully, we might talk to the manager, and to some of the workers and try to make sense of what we hear. This may sound like the third-party intervention of OD (Organisational Development) but in a fundamental way it is different because OD relates to an acceptance of the organisation as such being the key element, a "disembodied reality." From a phenomenological stand point organisational significance may or may not be relevant. What the phenomenologist is trying to do is simply to make sense of the situation, not to change it — though he knows it will change.

Is, then, a phenomenological organisation theorist a theorist at all? Is simply anyone entitled to propound organisation theories? Initially, the answer must be yes — since any interpretation must be 'valid' for the interpreter. The onus for understanding is always on the interpreter next in line, and the essential requirements for making valid subjective interpretations are:

1. awareness of one's own value system
2. ability to think logically and abstractly
3. consciously remembered experience of organisations and people's behaviour in them.

The material form in which data about organisations occurs is in some kind of narrative — spoken or written; documentation used within the organisation and outside it but about it; rituals practised in the organisation; projections from individuals in the organisation to those seen to be outside (e.g. advertising, publicity, communications). To make sense of data of this nature an individual requires the sort of training an historian, a literary and dramatic critic, an anthropologist, a psychiatrist might have. Which is a long way from the social-psychology, political economy, operations research training, most organisation theorists appear to have.

Do organisations have objectives or purposes?

A penomenological perspective takes issue with much tranditional organisation theory at the point of definition of an organisation. Our definition so far will be totally unacceptable to many people who have a view about organisations, especially economists, political philosophers, financial experts, operations researchers and the general public who think they know what an organisation is. The phenomenologist is not concerned whether in itself an organisation is closely or loosely defined because he takes the definition from the definer. But he also goes further than this because he makes certain 'phenomenological' assumptions or values. Most definitions of organisations assume some sense of objectives or shared objectives, and this is an assumption the phenomenologist cannot share. To the phenomenologist, organisations serve purposes – that is, they exist to further the objectives of individuals but they have no objectives themselves. In fact, it is incorrect to speak of objectives since objectives require a conscious defining of activity outcome and evaluation and few, if any, 'objectives' can ever be clearly defined because objectives can only exist in a defined situation and no situation can be properly defined in advance of its arrival. (Objectives exist only as projections into the future but derive from an interpretation of the *present*). Individuals have hopes, wishes, needs, understandings, values, expectations and all of these are worked out through the organisation of which each is a member; hence organisations serve the purposes of individuals. For this reason no closer definition of an organisation is possible than that they are the experience of individuals who perceive them as organisations of whatever kind.

Because the phenomenological definition of an organisation is particular to itself, most of the other aspects of organisations which other theories take for granted or as given, are not perceived as having the same significance as is customary. For example, (phenomenologically) reward is perceived as having meaning only to individuals who perceive and evaluate 'reward' not in terms of what the "organisation" can offer. The idea of collective bargaining and uniform salaries takes on a different meaning if it is seen as part of an individual bargaining process by some members for their own personal satisfaction rather than the seeking of an acceptable reward for all recipients. Furthermore reasons for collective behaviour are seen to be much more complex than many political interpretations give them credit for. The emphasis that a phenomenological approach gives is towards understanding the meaning for individuals of their membership rather than trying to understand the organisation as a technological entity. On the other hand, phenomenology has to take into account the fact that most people *think* of organisations as having a separate and superior existence, that organisations exist in their own right, and that people behave on such premises.

What is organisational structure?

There appear to be three levels at which organisations can be described. The level of individual participation, the level of technical structure, and the level of the organisation as an abstract entity. Most organisation theory has been concerned with technical structure; even the sociological concern with problems of role, leadership, power and authority are essentially structural in concern while all the administrative approaches are overtly structure-conscious. The concern is for better or more effective patterns of communication, improving the use of resources, developing relationships in teams and so forth. Quantitative aspects of organisations are, by their very nature structure-conscious and of course their structure is preoccupied with the technology of the quantitative process not the quantity of the inter-relationships of people. The concept of structure is problematic in organisation theory because though structure is a function of task performance (i.e. structure is the way the performance of a task can be described), structures tend to continue beyond the task needs, and to be continued into different tasks, while some theorists appear to believe that there are ideal (or at least good/better) structures which can be imposed on new situations. A phenomenologist would be unable to *pre*scribe a structure for a situation but would wait for one to emerge. In practice no formal, legally constituted organisation can be set up without a "structure" being put forward but such a structure is notional not real; it is only activated when people begin to interact. The levels at which the organisation actually functions are not the technical (or 'structural') level at all but the two other levels of personal involvement and perceived organisational identity. Functioning on the technical level is also personal rather than mechanical. For instance, even in a chemical process plant where the structure appears to be inherent in the process, the levels of individual functioning and organisational perception are human activities not disembodied processes. Individuals cause strikes, stoppages and absences while the ascribed identity to the organisation induces customers to buy the product, consider the firm reliable, to value the training given to operatives and so on.

While it is comparatively straightforward to examine the ways individuals think of the organisation — by using an analytic interview technique, it is more difficult to understand organisations as "entities." We need a basic theory or perspective to describe organisation that is compatible with our theory of people in organisations. If the phenomenological view is that an organisation is what its members perceive or believe it to be, then from both inside and outside any organisation is "perceived to be" in some way or another. If I believe a store to be expensive and snobbish, then I shall tend to behave accordingly and may or may not change my opinion whatever my experience. But if the staff at the store perceives that I perceive the store as expensive and snobbish they too will respond accordingly. And if they, for the most part, wish the store to have such an image, so it will stand a good chance of being so perceived by more people. In this way, the collective nature of an organisation consolidates certain dispositions and these dispositions are essentially psychological so that the organisation as an "entity" exists in a psychological state. There is empirical evidence that organisations have a psychological dimension which is generalised and embracing. As we mention names of large companies or small shops, a consciousness of the 'image' of that company or shop arises in the mind but the matter goes further than this. Organisations sometimes seem to take on some of the characteristics of individual personality. If we examine churches, some have a 'death wish' and go into decline while others change and adapt. Some organisations behave defensively and aggressively and organisations like the CIA appear to be positively paranoic. Such images probably derive from the characteristics of leading individuals.

The psychology of organisations

It seems logical, that if we look at organisations from a psychological* viewpoint, that perspective should apply equally well to examining the organisation as an entity as looking at it as a collection of individuals with varying degrees of sensitivity to the larger organisation. The techniques for understanding organisations by reference to individuals are beginning to come clear; the techniques for understanding organisations in their completeness may well be an extension of the individual methods but are less clear. The most useful way of understanding how an individual perceives an organisation is by an unstructured depth interview. The investigator, researcher or consultant talks at length to an individual to find out how the individual sees himself, and how he perceives himself in the organisation. Various interview techniques and approaches are employed deriving from counselling, psychotherapy and encounter group situations. Interviews may also be group interviews, but they are not therapeutic or psychiatric unless the investigator is acting officially as a consultant to the

* Historically, clinical psychology has been essentially phenomenological in whatever tradition it has followed.

organisation; in this latter case his roll will be to create a helping relationship in an action-research kind of intervention and T-groups, and encounter groups may be used as a means of providing feedback to organisation members themselves. From interviews, a picture of the psychology of the organisation will emerge so that if many individuals feel that the organisation does not value people, some kind of overall view becomes clear which may have implications for the senior staff or boss.

A phenomenological standpoint is useful in examining the problems that arise from planning. Planning is notoriously unable to account for the unexpected yet the unexpected (nearly) always happens. Planning is done on the basis of projections based on data, but the selection of data is dependent upon the experience of the planner and his ability to extrapolate from the past. It is impossible to anticipate all eventualities and currently good planning tries *to provide for* the unexpected. The emphasis, however, is more on providing for something that is going to happen, rather than coping with something that has already happened; for example with critical path analysis, PPBS, PERT and so forth. An alternative 'hand to mouth' approach is unacceptable in an industrialised culture: it is seen as the view that 'what will be, will be'. Phenomenology would be more positive. It would recognise the difficulty of knowing all the future, but recognise that in practice much in the future can largely be anticipated and predicted where that future is largely concerned with routine and ritual. However, a phenomenological perspective leads to an emphasis on skills at coping with situations as they happen and creates a functional caution over planning expectation. By adopting a phenomenological stance, the real questions of planning become clearer and can be dealt with in a different way and provision made more carefully for coping with the unexpected.

The validity of subjectivity

There are three areas in which the validity of an organisation theory must be tested—coherence and consistency of the theoretical construct, the applicability of the construct to the situations which it claims to explain, and the devising of relevant research techniques to support the theoretical hypotheses. At the present time, it is in the area of relevant research procedures that there is greatest need. Research approaches are likely to derive from psychotherapy, philosophical analysis, social anthropology, literary criticism rather than the natural and mathematical sciences. Bizarre and eclectic though these sources may seem, they have the advantage of being much concerned, overtly with the question of personal values. Up to this present time the history of social and organisational analysis has been an attempt to prove its scientific credibility but in so doing the wrong techniques have been used. The rational sciences may aim to be value free – the social sciences cannot avoid values.

3.
Organisations as
Subjectives

The purpose of this paper is to suggest a new basis for a general model of organisations by which we can examine what is happening in an educational institution. A model is simply a way of describing in a coherent and systematic way what happens in the organisation and of expressing the ways in which various parts relate to one another. All models make basic assumptions which amount to a 'perspective' and naturally no model can account for all the phenomena that go to make up an organisation. To be useful, a model must be capable of being understood and interpreted by a reasonably informed reader and not so complex as to be unmanageable by him. The basic assumption behind the model presented here is that organisations function in terms of the understanding of them that members bring to them and that the problems of organisations arise as each member acts on his own perceptions which are in greater or lesser degree not shared by (i.e. are incongruent with) those of other members. This model presents a psychological view of organisations in that its concern is with the psychological aspects of the people who are members of the organisation.

We may describe an organisation as a 'collective fantasy' in that each member behaves on the basis of assumptions he makes and these assumptions are never fully tested and confirmed both because there is never time or need to test them and also because the situation to which the assumptions refer changes once the assumptions are acted on. Furthermore, behaviour in organisations generally *anticipates* consequences rather than responds to conditions; that is to say, most behaviour of members of organisations is based on assumptions about what is going to happen rather than what has 'actually' occurred. The fallacy of human organisation theory is to assume that members of an organisation respond in the same way as material physical phenomena occur (for example, as the response of electric current to the completion of a circuit). Human behaviour is normally and usually anticipative in some measure. Hence what we are largely concerned with in organisations is not a series of expected *responses* but a sequence of *anticipative* behaviours. Because what is anticipated never happens, organisations consist of patterns of largely disconnected behaviour. We may offer the hypothesis that the ability of an organisation to change and adapt depends on its developing ways of permitting members to behave in unexpected ways and to cope well with other members' unexpected behaviour.

We need to define the concept of fantasy more precisely. Broadly speaking, the term is used as in Gestalt Psychology by Frederick Perls and is not used here pejoratively. Fantasy for each individual is the operational aspect of his interpretation of 'reality'. For each individual,

39

of course, his fantasy may be his 'reality' and I use the term to indicate the existence of a multiplicity of 'realities'. Whether there be a 'Platonic' reality or not does not concern us operationally though there may well be an 'actuality' that several members of an organisation see in almost the same way — though it can never be "the same". 'Fantasy' is the experience each of us has of a situation: for example, each reader of this paper experiences it differently and ascribes different 'meanings' to it. (We could test that by asking the question, 'Why are you reading this paper?' Each answer would be in some way different and some of these differences would be significant depending upon the depth with which we explored the answers). Individual fantasies are the expression of the perceptions of reality that each person experiences. Fantasies are dynamic and not just snapshop views of the organisation. They range from quite personal experiences of the organisation that relate largely to the individual — such as whether he finds his room congenial and physically comfortable — to shared fantasies* such as a suspicion of student associations. The further we move away from the individual towards the 'organisation' the more complex will be the incongruities among members' perceptions. We may be able to deal with one member's fantasies about the comfort of his room by changing the furniture but when we look at the discontent about the organisation felt by all the teaching faculty, we find as many complexities of reasons as there are people and no two will coincide exactly. (It is theoretically possible that reasons do coincide but the odds are enormous when we remember how complex reasons are in pragmatic terms. Simple responses like "feeling too hot" may be so nearly congruent as to be effectively congruent.)

Each member of the organisation makes his assumptions about other members and develops a number of expectations which are evaluative. For example teachers may assume that students wish to learn, and select and evaluate the types of learning behaviour they will accept. Students who do not fulfil these expectations are evaluated positively or negatively but generally negatively — for example, students who exceed expectations may make life uncomfortable for the teacher by making him work harder than he wishes. As members work through their fantasies they evaluate the outcomes, and evaluation determines their future response to the organisation — setting up a new set of expectations based on a new set of assumptions.

---

* We should call these collective fantasies or fantasy sets or fantasy clusters to acknowledge that each individual's fantasies differ in some measure.

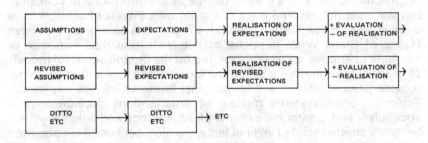

All the time, each individual interprets what goes on not only in terms of his understanding of his experience but in terms of his own personality needs. That is to say, he interprets what happens in the organisation in terms of his own personality and also in terms of his current general needs and life experience. Whatever system of personality types* we adopt, the evidence suggests that personality determines likes and preferences. Extraverts will tend to view organisations differently from introverts and will certainly have different requirements of organisations. Additionally, current life experience will modify the personality view so that an extravert of 44 years of age will view the organisation differently from an extravert aged 24 because the process of maturity will have taught different ways of satisfying his needs.

This is a highly complex view of organisations and yet the implications are very important. If each individual perceives an organisation differently and has different needs of the organisation, does that affect the basic organisation? Surely, it may be argued, individual differences are marginal and organisations function success-fully in much cruder terms. The question can only be answered by examining further the concepts of fantasy, reality and actuality, and also the concept of organisation and institution.

---

* All theories of personality have implications for organisational behaviour. For instance, Jungian theories of types lead to assumptions about behaviour matching. See, for example, the personality types developed by Isabel Briggs Myers, "Introduction to Type" Centre for Applications of Psychological Type 1962 etc.

The operation of collective fantasy may or may not involve compromise, and/or collusion. The idle fantasies of patients in a mental hospital who each live in their own nearly totally separate worlds do not involve much, if any, compromise beyond the physical. In normal organisations, there is a greater degree of compromise and collusion, but we must not assume there is a great deal. Heads of schools have been known to live in their own private world as comfortably as have Heads of State. What happens is that each individual imposes, or attempts to impose, a fantasy structure on the organisation. All models of organisations impose a simplified fantasy structure and in so doing, provide a vocabulary in which personal fantasies may be expressed. Typically, open systems models of organisations provide such a vocabulary and grammar — a matrix of terminology and linkages which becomes another level or layer of fantasy which, because it is a common language for members, permits fantasies to be worked out at the level of a *game*. This is what almost all management "theory" has been about — an analysis of the organisational "game". Games, of course, work perfectly well in their own terms — again, the open systems model of organisations illustrates this; so do financial and economic models of organisations. These technical models may well be "useful" (in fact, they *are* useful since no organisation can exist without them), but they cannot supply us with the information that is most crucial to any organisation's functioning — how people behave and are going to behave — except in the grossest impersonal terms (for example, that a certain number of positions will be needed if the company is to increase production). A typical technical model is PPBS (Planned Programmed Budgetting System) which deludes people into certain beliefs about the organisation in terms of goals and financing.

The imposition of a technical model on an organisation is itself the imposition of a fantasy construct which still is open to subjective interpretation by everyone it affects. For example, a status structure (hierachy) may be quite satisfactory to the President of a company and his deputies, but totally unacceptable to members at a certain level who feel that their position has been undervalued. Conversely, members may impose a hierarchy the senior managers themselves do not accept. Subsequent behaviour will be critical for the organisation and is a consequence of member perception — not the boss' — nor the employees'. To cope with the situation, the perspective on the model has to be changed, the vocabulary altered. The meaning of the alteration does not lie in the model as such but in the meaning of the member's behaviour. We can only understand how individuals understand organisations at the point of contact with the individual; there is no such thing as contact with the organisation except in personal terms.

Bargaining and compromise are characteristics of the organisation at all levels but at the game level the behaviour is ritualised. Organisations generally function at the game level. Unfortunately, people change the rules and change the game while they are playing and do not always tell the other players. If we are properly to understand how organisations change, we need to go beyond the game level. If we centre on the Head alone, we may manage to explain the game and to some extent to understand it but never completely. The boss is not the only one to be changing the game and there is never anything in the game as it is played to indicate where the changes will come from. It is sometimes thought that trends can be identified as forces with clear directional paths. Certainly it seems that outsiders can identify change directions by analogy with similar organisations before organisation members can,* but organisations tend not to respond to outsiders' opinions. While technical models may flash warnings, they do not indicate how behaviour changes can take place because individuals have to make an internal, (mental), decision, and they do this subjectively, not objectively.

We still need to stay with the fantasy concept. It seems that the only *dynamic* about which we can be certain in organisations has to do with the "actuality" of "fantasy". The ultimate (and primary) need of an organisation is that (for each individual member) it has the purpose of providing a location or arena for fantasy needs. That is to say, the ultimate function of the organisation is to provide occasion for the working out of personal fantasies that derive from personal needs. Whatever else the organisation might do, the *critical* function is to fulfil the needs of members. Some models will describe things differently — for instance, an economic model will describe the ultimate function in terms of resources and products. But if we look carefully at organisations, we can see that members are interested basically not in what the organisation does in a material sense, but what it does in an emotional (*affective*) sense. Studies of churches,† for example, have shown that members are influenced by subjective sentiment more than anything else when changes in organisation are called for. Few shareholders care about the product of a company so long as the dividends are satisfactory. If we are to have a useful and operational theory of organisations, we must discard the ones that have only face validity and we must fall back on a phenomenological theory because that is the only approach that will generate an understanding that can be applied

---

* At least it is commonly thought so; consultants certainly believe this.
† See, for instance, an unpublished study (1971) by the author of a church dealing with a major change. Similar studies by the Grubb Institute indicate likewise.

to the basic management of the organisation. The phenomenological perspective declares that meaning is subjective, that individuals put their own interpretation on situations and act on the basis of that interpretation. I have called that subjective interpretation "fantasy" and can now explain how it applies to understanding organisations.

No model of an organisation tells us anything about the head as a person, however well it may describe the behaviour expected of the position. We all know how no two incumbents of a position behave in the same way. Individual behaviour is part of the dynamic of the organisation; the description of the position is not. Abstract descriptions of organisations are simply metaphors, often extended metaphors, but symbolic language nevertheless — such as the explanation of an organisation as a "machine" with interlocking parts. To understand "structure", we have to understand how people "actually"* behave. Structure is simply a description of actual or observed behaviour. Members of organisations have to cope from minute to minute with changes. The changes originate in the individual though they may be sparked off by changes in other individuals. There are no means of predicting behaviour except in terms of personal patterns of behaviour. In practice, we both do this and do not do this. We do it when it is convenient and we do not when it is difficult or inconvenient. (Most likely in regular practice we have things the wrong way round and we assume predictability when the situation is easy and unpredictability when things are difficult). This is where managers make their mistakes because they prefer to act quickly and make decisions as simply as possible. Technical models encourage this approach. But it should be recalled that the more significant the change, the greater the emotional involvement of each member and the more personal and less organisational his concern will be. In a company threatened with bankruptcy, individuals are more concerned with their personal futures than the concerns of the company. There is no way in which company concerns can supplant personal ones however much the head may consider company interests to be paramount.

The importance of understanding organisations as subjectivities is that we can deal with the fundamental aspects of organisational functioning and we can place the organisation in its psycho-sociological and socio-economic context. For example, we can describe an educational institution in technical terms and relate these to social and economic developments. For many purposes such

---

* So as not to be sidetracked into the casuistry of meanings, we understand "actual" to be that which is "acted on" or that which is observed.

descriptions are useful — for instance, so far as local authority provision of school places is concerned (considering demographic projections and so on). However, the functions of the school in the psychological context of its members and the community to which it belongs means that the true forces of influence on the school depend on the realisation of a good many personal demands and needs. The school may have a symbolic meaning for the community as a prestigious, scholarly institution. For the head, it may be the opportunity to fulfil his educational ideals. For teachers, it may offer important career stages. For pupils, a guarantee of certain desired post-school situations. For the population at large, it will have a variety of social, political and economic significances. And so on. If we are to understand how the school copes with change, we have to examine not the technical model of the educational institution (for instance, the basis of the local authority funding), but the personal needs of individuals for whom the school is a critical symbol and arena for achievement. At one level, this is to describe the political significance of organisations, but more funamentally, it is to describe the psychology of such politics.

If organisations are so subjective, how do different perceptions relate? Surely organisations are not anarchies? There appears to be order, coherence and relationship in practice. How can organisations have both objective and subjective "reality"? Such is just the basic management dilemma so that management can "in reality" be no more than the coordination of separate fantasies.

For the most part, the fantasies that we have about organisations are restrictive. We create our fantasies in order to best cope with the organisation as it impinges upon us. We look for justification of what we want to do and express it, if we can, altruistically. A department head calls lots of meetings because his means of coping requires a close relationship of such a kind with his colleagues. He finds justification for his behaviour — his personal means of coping — by creating a model of the organisation; say an authoritarian model. So long as his colleagues share a similar model, the situation accommodates all of them equally well. Where colleagues work on a different model, there will be conflict and dysfunctional* behaviour. The more important/significant an organisation is to an individual, the more open or closed will be his fantasy model according to the degree of personal threat he perceives. The less threat he perceives, the more open to change will he be.

---

* In this context 'dysfunctional' is a problematic term!

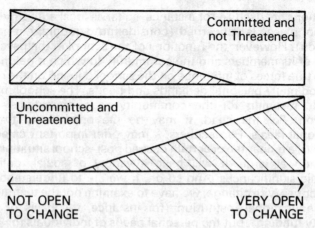

Committed and
not Threatened

Uncommitted and
Threatened

←————————————————————————→
NOT OPEN   VERY OPEN
TO CHANGE   TO CHANGE

Change is dependent on reduced threat to individuals but what constitutes security will be personal and unique. If in general a threat is a perceived potential deprivation, then the contrary must be a perceived promise of reward. A proferred reward must be at least equal to the current reward and to be effective must be more than the current reward if it is to be an inducement to change. We may take as axiomatic that an individual only changes when he perceives the promised return to be *greater* than the current return; equilibrium is no inducement. We may state the hypothesis that change occurs in an institution when the rewards as perceived by individuals exceed the current rewards. There will be a critical 'mass' of membership that determines the degree of collective or organisational change. Clearly this is determined subjectively. Whatever the material base, the return is psychological. A second hypothesis is that resistance to change occurs when the promised return is perceived as less than the current return. Such resistance will be activated into opposition according to the way in which an individual feels threatened. Thus it is apparent that the management of organisations on gross generalisations about returns to individuals (self-interest) is open to gross distortion in unpredictable ways. This mistake of management has been to view members as belonging to large classes of people with identical interests and to relate to them crudely. A good example is the way colleges deal with student activists, generally assuming that they represent the whole student body though they can come to represent a complex of varying discontents of individual students. Discontented groups are only too often scape-goats for other managerial problems.

By definition, formal organisations define positions, roles and rewards and lay down procedures for processes. They are designed as snap-shot models. During the process of becoming established, contracts are worked out in terms of this snap-shot. However, this status represents a base for bargaining by members and not an accepted stationary situation. In practice, members seek for changes that will give greater 'returns'. All activity in the organisation comes to be concerned with individuals trying to improve their own position for bargaining in order to fulfil their fantasy concepts of the organisation. Management is the function of facilitating this, if rightly understood – not determining or even controlling it. Hence management is a function of all members, not just those designated to be in management positions. In fact, those in 'control' positions are in exactly the same negotiating situation as other members. Rather than attempting to reinforce their power and status, they would be more functionally effective if they concentrated on the facilitating of others' need achievement.*

A theory of organisations as arenas for fantasy realisation moves the emphasis for mangement away from a concentration on inert 'structure' as an "objective fact" of organisational life to an emphasis on the *processes* which occur in an organisation, specifically the bargaining process whereby individuals seek to support their fantasies. For example, we can look at the way the head seeks to satisfy his personel needs in the position of head. If his behaviour is functional, he will realise his needs without depriving others of their freedom to achieve but if it is dysfunctional he will simply attempt to retain power and control by rewards and coercion – by methods which may be totally unnecessary for his personal needs for esteem and approval.

There may be a tendency for those high in the hierarchy to identify with the organisation in personal terms, so that they see complete identity between themselves and the organisation. Identification of this sort is exceedingly common and presents considerable problems. Bosses tend to convert personal goals into organisational goals, endowing them with an infallible objectivity. Young organisations receive their momentum from this identification† but it becomes increasingly unrealistic as the organisation grows older. Heads come to speak of 'my school' and industrial bosses believe that no one can have company interests so much at heart as they do. The higher the executive position, the greater the tendency for personal goals to be viewed as organisational goals. Organisations cannot in themselves have goals because people are required for the achievement of goals. At best

---

* We can understand this concept of the management function if we study the function of leadership as it occurs in small group theory.
† Most typically in charismatic organisations experience of an organisation centres on ourself in association with other groups and pairings.

organisational 'goals' are vehicles for personal goals, at worst they are mirages. This is true also of technical processes which serve the needs of individuals — for instance, a chocolate factory may have members who never eat chocolates. While the goal of the factory is to produce chocolate, 'production' is the process whereby members achieve personal satisfactions. In a crisis, the question is what do the members need, not what should the organisation do. This is true of material crises. It needs to be understood that crises are never essentially 'material' but the consequence of managerial perceptions*.

A psychological model of an organisation is more difficult to construct than a technological one. Furthermore, unlike a complex piece of equipment (like a computor) there is no need to compile a complete one since organisations begin to function as soon as two people come together. The kind of model we need in order to understand an organisation is an experiential one and as such it is different in kind from the mechanical models most management text books appear to prefer. An experiential model is simply the sum of one's experience of an organisation with whatever insights and understandings follow from the experience. Each of us experiences an organisation in a personal way as an individual, as a member of a group of individuals, and as a member of a group relating to other groups and individuals.

We can construct a model for organisational behaviour based on research into the behaviour of people in groups and I have developed such descriptive models elsewhere.† Here we are concerned with the individual interpretation of observed and experienced behaviour and the attribution of value to that behaviour. For instance, an individual may observe that leadership is shared among three members of a group of six and this observation may be verified by outside observers. But we cannot know the meaning and significance attributed to that changing pattern of leadership until we have questioned closely the members whose response we are interested in. While it is possible to observe physical behaviour it is not possible to observe psychological reactions, even though we may guess at them. It is the evaluated behaviour of people in organisations that is important if we are to understand the how and why of change.

---

* Whatever happens in the organisation, each individual is, so far as he himself is concerned, always central and he views everything from his own point of view. No one is in any better position than anyone else to know what is going on though some will share more critical experiences than others. A critical experience is one that brings about change and some members will be concerned in more of these than others.

† See Chapter 4.

The implication of the foregoing is that another dimension must be added to management if it is to cope with the origins of change influences. The addition of another management structure or 'technique' is not required — such would simply be an extension of the Administrative Model which sets up secretariats to deal with every new idea. Rather the implications are two-fold. On the one hand, the necessity for much management activity is brought into question because most management activity is an extension of personal needs rather than real necessity. On the other hand, managers must recognise that it is the interests of members that must receive attention and not mythical abstractions like 'education', 'progress', 'profitability' or whatever. Such terms are phrases used by managers in justification of their own needs and preferences. This is not to say that organisations ought to be inward-looking, self-interested institutions but rather to emphasise that unless rewards are perceived to come to members, they have no cause to wish for the success or continued existence of the organisation. Not surprisingly, when the chips are down, the main concern of an organisation is to preserve itself only until the senior members have secured satisfactory alternate employment. In the process, many are shocked to discover that they were neither so 'senior' nor highly valued as they thought. In practice, material and technical aspects of organisations are always secondary to and dependent on personal aspects.

The argument appears to be in favour of much better communication among members of an organisation but not communication in the generally understood sense of information dissemination. Rather it implies a particular kind of personal relationship among members where feelings and perceptions are shared at a deep and personal level. Not many senior executives give themselves time for this, preferring the various political games offered by the organisation. For most managers a change of management style is required alongside a revaluation of personal goals.

An understanding of organisations from the psychological perspective described here does not lead us to suggest a wholesale restructuring of organisations. There is no likelihood, for instance, that educational institutions will change radically in form and purpose nor even in structure — if only because vested interests are too strong. But a change in management style throughout the organisation is both necessary and possible. This style change requires a movement away from a concern with administrative *procedures* to behavioural processes. The shift is from a power-coercive or political approach which characterises most formally constituted meetings in organisations to a process facilitating approach which releases the creativity of conflict

49

resolution. Instead of trying to suppress conflict, the leadership function is concerned with resolving conflict by helping colleagues to work through their positions by facing up to and coming to understand personal viewpoints. Individuals will be helped to uncover and come to terms with the fantasies they have about themselves. Since designated leaders have fantasies in the same way as other members, leadership roles must revolve. The first critical decision of established management would be to open up the opportunity for shared leadership—though this is a personal threat few managers can face. In practice, top management may need to retain a traditional position but to encourage change within the organisation by a judicious encouragement of initiative at points where potential creativity can be observed — outside help being necessary. If senior managers consider one of the major functions of all managers to be training colleagues in management, there is chance of some progress towards gradual change and not calamity.

The importance of understanding organisations as collective subjectivities is both theoretical and practical. If we can remember that individuals behave in a highly individualistic and self-centred way we come near to understanding how organisations function. This understanding leads to certain appropriate coping behaviours. But additionally, it enables us to appreciate the true nature of what are generally considered the objective aspects of organisations — the very misunderstandings that lead to organisational collapse in the commercial and economic spheres. Economic and financial models are as much fantasy as any other perspectives on organisations but because of the Western worship of the material world, physical things have been given an undue precedence over the non-material. A phenomenological theory gives an opportunity to redress the balance and points a way towards better coping.

4.
Training People to Understand Organisations: a Clinical Approach

There are two problems about helping people to understand behaviour in organisations. The first is the lack of an adequate theory of organisations and the second is the need for a satisfactory pedagogic theory. The first of these tasks concerns organisation theory and an attempt to deal with this has been an important preoccupation of many involved in management education in recent years.* In this paper an attempt is made to explain the theory and practice of an experiential mode of learning about organisational behaviour developed between 1970 and the present time.

The organisation theory which underlies the teaching approach to be described here takes the basic assumption that organisations are essentially creations of their members and that they function in response to the ways their members understand them. This view derives from a phenomenological standpoint which considers the most significant understanding about organisations to come from the perceptions and understanding of members and those others who consider the organisation. The phenomenological view would be that each member of an organisation creates his own realities for that organisation. However else we may describe a school the most important leads to understanding come from the descriptions of members, which indicate how they behave in the school. This is why two schools with the same overt "structure" have quite different "ethos", behavioural and relational patterns among members and users. In other words, the key to understanding an organisation arises from an examination of how its members understand it.

Virtually all attempts to develop a theory of organisations† have so far been concerned to provide an abstract and consistent "model", or series of models, of organisations in terms of which all organisations can be understood. So far as some aspects of organisations are concerned such an approach may well have validity, at least where those aspects are tangible, quantitative and do in fact have causal connection. Because human behaviour in organisations is not adequately predictable and is not directly causal, so much organisation theory of late has been concerned with motivation in one form or another (e.g. leadership, decision making, problem solving, communication). These aspects are matters of attitudes and values not essential parameters of organisational structure. Furthermore, no description of the technical structure of an organisation can reveal what actually happens only

---

* Most "organisation theory" appears to be about 'work groups' within industrial, military, or public service 'organisations'.

† With the possible exception of D. Silverman; The Theory of Organisations. Heineman, London 1970.

what, at best, was what one hoped would happen. Yet any valid theory of organisations must, by definition, help us to understand what "actually" happens even if actuality means different things to different people. A clinical viewpoint accepts that there is no one reality and a multiplicity of viewpoints and experiences must be taken heed of if any proper understanding is to be achieved.

Other theories of organisation have assumed that organisations can be understood by examination from outside. Maybe a "researcher" armed with a schedule, a model or instruments of measurement visits the organisation and attempts to understand what he sees or observes.* Or he may collect "data" and then attempt to make scientifically valid deductions. All of these theories rest on the assumption that what is apparent on the surface is much the same as, or relates closely to, what lies underneath. A different approach might assume that what was observed, while an indication of something underlying, was not itself the same as the underlying phenomenon. This is the approach of clinical psychology which takes the "presenting" problem as no more than an indicator that further problems have to be dealt with.

There are other reasons why a clinical approach to organisation appears to be more satisfactory than the *a priori* model approach. For one thing, "models" tend to produce the kind of problem they are set up to find whether they exist or not. Secondly, no model can be comprehensive yet in dealing with problems in organisations we are forced to deal with the "real" problem not the one that is convenient. Thirdly, models are remarkably value-laden — which is all right if one shares the values or if the values are declared. On the other hand, an experiential viewpoint forces the researcher to find and deal with *other people's* reality not his own version. In practice this means his clinical stand-point is not to find justification for his own interpretations but to seek to understand the interpretations of others who actually belong to the organisation. This is by no means to claim that a clinical approach is value free — far from it — but a clinical approach seeks to recognize the values of the members as well as those of the interpreter. It accepts the validity of values and subjectivity, uses this recognition as a strength, and does not pretend that objectivity is an attainable ideal.

If we take a clinical approach to organisations, most of the customary research techniques are not relevant or even valid. Collecting "data" about such matters as "organisational climate," preferred leadership styles, communication patterns and so on, is an irrelevant activity since no broad conclusions can be derived from

‡ e.g. the Aston School—Pugh *et al;* Organisation Theory. Penguin, Hamondsworth. 1971.

such conglomerate material. Even if we can indicate a climate as "democratic" we still need to know how each individual understands "democratic" and furthermore how he behaves in a "democratic" climate. The crux of understanding is knowledge of individuals not collectivities — the behaviour of collectivities is another aspect of phenomenological behaviour.

The behaviour of people in organisations can be observed on several levels. How we describe these levels is a matter of perspective and no paradigm is exclusive. Paradigms are merely ways by which we help ourselves and others to make sense of what we observe (or to enable us to observe in categories and classes). Generally, paradigms suggest "pure types" of category even though pure types never exist.* If we must use paradigms they may as well be generalities that obviously are vague, rather than apparently precise descriptions which delude us into believing that they exist. John F. Morris uses a vague general paradigm of organisational levels when he describes behaviour on the three levels of routine, ritual and drama; an idea interesting enough to excite but not precise enough to deceive us into believing that it says all there is to say about levels of behaviour. In our clinical view of organisations we posit three levels of behaviour —

Political: This is the level of power-seeking and power-redistribution and is the level on which most organisations overtly function. There are rules and rituals (norms) for political behaviour, the main objective of which is to gain more power for oneself.

Social: This is the level of normative, consensus-seeking, peer-related behaviour. It is the social organisation concerned with polite, non-confronting behaviour which maintains the power status-quo.

Psychological: This is the level of the hidden agendas, the level of personal motivation and need; it is the level of hidden reasons for actions.

Organisations function superficially on the three levels alternating between the first and second according to the nature of the situation. But if we really wish to know why things are happening we need to work at the psychological level where we have a chance of discovering

---

* For example, Etzioni's model of nine pure types of "compliance".

why people behave as they do. This we cannot do by observation* alone but only by interaction with members of the organisation. The type of interaction which we describe here, we call "clinical" because it resembles in many ways medical and psycho-analytic diagnosis. That is to say, although the diagnostician has a medical or psycho-analytic framework which determines his diagnosis, his primary concern is to obtain information that will help him to interpret the meaning of the symptoms or data. The more skilled a diagnostician, the less readily will he seek a common solution. The clinical situation essentially involves full participation by diagnostician and each member of the organisation. The diagnostic framework preferred by the present writer is that of Gestalt psychology† in that the concern is with "healthy" people who are members of organisations as complete individuals, not aspects of 'personality' such as "schizophrenics" or "paranoics,"; not as "head-masters" or "teachers," but as whole people occupying organisational positions.

If one takes a clinical perspective of organisations the teaching and the training problem are very closely allied. An individual's theories of organisation derive from his personal understanding of organisational behaviour. That is, he learns to make sense of organisations *for himself.* In practice, organisations are too large and one's involvement too pressing for teaching about organisations and work to go on side by side so an *experimental* situation has to be set up. The experimental situation is the small group (usually of from 8 to 25 members) which engages in an *experiential* mode of learning; a modified form of T-Group — sometimes called an Organisation Development Group because the purpose is to examine how an organisation develops. The learning process involved, however, may be quite costly and time-consuming.

The Organisation Development Group is totally *experiential* in that it is quite "unstructured." That is to say, it is a form of Encounter or Sensitivity Group with the task of helping members to understand organisations by examining the behaviour of the group. There are two focusses: on the individual himself who is helped to understand himself in the group and his behaviour outside the group; and also on the group as an "organisation" where the members have psychological bonding. (Nowadays, the term T-Group has no more precise meaning than any

---

* In spite of all the popular books about making deductions about behaviour from what we appear to observe — Body Language, etc., — social anthropologists do not all corroborate their data.

† See Perls, F. *et al.:* Gestalt Therapy. Dell Publishing Co. Inc. N.Y. 1951.

other teaching term and will have to be understood in context in the description that follows.)

If the hypothesis is that organisations are what its members create in their own minds and that each of us reacts according to our understanding of "reality," then the purpose of the OD Group is to help the members to understand themselves as members of organisations. To do this, the "group" becomes the "organisation" and as the members explore what happens in the group so they better understand themselves as individuals and themselves as members of the group. The role of the Trainer (or Facilitator) is simply to facilitate this learning in whatever way he feels most competent. In this regard the role and behaviour of the Trainer is quite different from that of, for instance, Tavistock Trainers,* though the theories have much in common with Tavistock theories of organisations. From time to time, the Trainer will make brief "theory" inputs as he feels necessary though it is probably preferable for the groups to run in two parallel or interweaving sections, one in experience and one in theory. In some cases, developmental phases of group behaviour are clear but in other cases there appears to be comparatively little "development." Since clinical theory of organisations claims that while behaviour can be recognised when it occurs but predicted only in the broadest sense, lack of "development" in some groups is to be expected. In fact, the basis of clinical theory is that behaviour *cannot* be predicted, but only recognised when it occurs. What occurs will not be unexpected but that is not the same as being predicted. This is an important emphasis.

The major problem of group development is that of dependency†. Group members are totally dependent on the trainer not only for making sense of the group experience which is quite enigmatic but for approval of everything that happens. There is also dependency on one another as each seeks to discuss the acceptable behaviour patterns (norms) for the group. The group passes beyond the phases of dependency and counterdependency though it is believed subsequent phases are through group mutuality and support to autonomy and personal independence.‡ However, formal organisations seem seldom to progress beyond counterdependency so the learning opportunities in the experiential group are more extensive than in real life. Clinical theory suggests that dependency is one of the great behavioural variables in

---

* See Peter B. Smith: Groups in Organisations. Harper & Row 1973. pp 102–103.
† See W. R. Bion: "Experience in Groups." Tavistock London 1961.
‡ See Harvey, O. J. Hunt David E. & Schroder H. M.: Conceptual Systems and Personality Organisation, John Wiley, N.Y. 1961.

organisational behaviour and by exploring dependency and counter-dependency in the group, members obtain insight at the psychological level – insight that is quite personal and subjective because it arises from each individual's understanding of himself in the group situation.

As with a normal Encounter Group, behaviour can be divided into two classes: individual and group. Clinical theory takes notice especially of openness and owning up, of the talking through of personal problems followed by relief and closure, of catharsis, of the resistance of individuals to bringing their problems (with the group) to the group, and of withdrawal and opting out. All these are behaviours of people in organisations played out in routine or ritual patterns. Members of organisations find different ways of withdrawing and in the clinical groups ways of doing this can be observed and experienced. In the group learning situation, "feedback" is a technique for checking out on what happens and is believed to have happened. For most group members, the major effect of this experience is to make them question their interpretation of behaviour, make them aware of the dangers of interpretation, make them conscious of their assumptions, and to help them to look beyond what is presented on the surface.

Behaviours of the group, as a psychological collective that can be observed, are a general avoidance of important issues (that is, those which without being resolved will impede progress); resistance to change or development; displacement, or substitution by another topic or task, one which threatens to become difficult or dangerous; coasting or coming to a generally "good" mutuality or warm feelings; (and hence avoid the struggles necessary for progress); and listening and supporting. The *experimental* nature of the group permits this group behaviour to be examined in a fairly "pure" state, unspoilt by the routines and rituals of formal organisation. By examining these comparatively few phenomena of group development, individuals are able to commence the building of a theory of organisations based on their own experience, personal to them but open to caution in general application. Individuals trained in this way have begun a theory of organisations which enables them to re-interpret their other organisational experiences. As they build a coherent framework they have to accommodate the richness of the experiences and the experiences of others.

For each member, the organisation centres round himself. Most students on group training courses hold middle or senior-managerial positions and bring into the group a range of problems which become the concern of the group. Most groups turn out to be "peer groups" of one sort or another and the over-riding fear is to be found wanting in comparison with peers. Of course, the group situation creates anxiety but the anxieties appear to fall into a few non-pathological* categories. First is a sense of inadequacy in comparison with colleagues—others are perceived to be more able and competent in their equivalent work positions. Then there is a very common sense of failure often associated with guilt and generally parent-conditioned because even "obviously successful" people suffer from a strong sense of personal failure. Associated with this is fear of failure which seems to be socially conditioned. Ambition is another anxiety since so many people have frustrated ambition to succeed socially and in their job; this often seems a distorted form of natural ambition which can be satisfied in self-fulfilment or self-realisation. Often there are a large number of personal anxieties — quality of intelligence, many sexual problems, problems of personal identity (very common indeed). These problems are "dealt with" by the individual in the group by denial, projection, transference and sometimes successful coping. Members generally readily see how these personal anxieties are manifested in formal organisations by such behaviour as aggressiveness, laziness, punctiliousness, authoritarianism, inadequate performance and so on. In this way many "organisational" problems are seen for what they really are — transferences of personal problems into organisational terms. Using the experience of the group, it can be observed how most people experience conflict between role requirements and self-concepts and dispositions. Theoretically, organisational problems are personal problems expressed in special terms. The training concern is to show how individuals respond and behave as whole persons rather than just as aspects of the person. For example, a principal of a school is first of all a person—when he can accept himself as a full person he has no need to concern himself with role requirements (as distinct from job requirements).

Trainer techniques for clinical training derive from Gestalt and Rogerian psycho-therapy but are specific to this kind of training and demand an understanding of organisation theory as well as counselling techniques. Broadly, the clinical approach is a form of group counselling with theory inputs. A number of trainer behaviours seem to characterize the group, and they can be listed briefly. *Questioning* tends to be of a Gestalt type aimed at giving and receiving feedback. All learning in the group is primarily "affective" or at the emotional level because the assumption is that emotional acceptance is a precondition of cognitive learning. Group members are learning to "feel" about situations and then to check out their feelings before they make

---

* An assumption is that group members are normal and not in a pathological psychological condition. Group members should, of course, be screened.

substansive deductions. The trainer also provides *feedback* in terms of his reactive feelings to situations and individual behaviour. The trainer also *plays hunches* in order to help individuals to understand themselves—hunches are guesses used as starting points for discussion and are talked out with the individual to see if they make sense to him. *Silence* is used to help the group to surface deeper and more substantial problems. Members themselves learn to use silence for a number of purposes once they have overcome their fear of it. By allowing silence the trainer shares the initiative and risk-taking with the group even though often they do not want the responsibility. The trainer both *personalises* and *depersonalises* situations when individuals escape from the implications of situations by either refusing to admit a personal issue or by failing to make a proper interpretation. The trainer will also *probe* when he feels undue resistance as a defence against an "awareness" of a personal problem. Such behaviour depends on his informed intuition, and training in informed intuition is one of the objectives of the learning process. Fundamental to all this is a belief that the "presenting problem" is only the lead to the substantive problem. Groups and organisations "present" problems continually but members seldom know how to seek the real problem and resolve it. Finally, the trainer helps the members to build personal theories of organisations consistent with their experience and current knowledge of organisations at a theoretical and cognitive level.

The major problem in using a clinical situation concerns the ability of group members to "buy in" to the experience. Since much of what is going to occur must remain unclear and ambiguous, members are required to make an act of faith in committing themselves to the group experience. The process of "buying in" however, is a part of the process of the group, since "buying in" is always a condition of membership of organisations and a dynamic aspect of membership. Very occasionally a group member cannot "buy in" and as a consequence withdraws either physically or psychologically — though never without facing consider-able problems which, of course, cannot be resolved since they concern the group and can only be resolved in the group. More frequently members try to retain spectator membership (observer and non-participant). Where this is the result of honest caution the issue can be dealt with but where the "observer" tries to play games with or tricks on the group the results are more painful than anticipated.* Impediments to group progress centre around the question of "buying in"; a group

---

* Often people who have experienced Encounter or T-Groups try to repeat what they can remember of trainer behaviour; unfortunately such projective behaviour seldom, if ever, works.

cannot seriously get down to its work until everyone has "bought in". Many formal organisations, however, have the same problem continually — lack of member commitment because members cannot appreciate the rewards avilable.

By helping people through an experience of a group — and eventually several experiences of several groups — in a clinical experience where members bring their own biases and perspectives and subject them to close scrutiny at both affective and cognitive levels, the trainer hopes to help his students to a personally valid and pragmatic understanding of organisational behaviour. The way is open for fuller descriptions of individual organisations and new approaches to research into organisations and scientific-academic credibility can be creatively developed. If organisations are what people perceive them to be, we can only come to understand them through understanding how we create our own perspectives, create our own worlds. If we can dig beneath the veneer of surface structure into the deep causal behaviour, then we at least stand a chance of discovering an adequate theoretical basis for organisation study and analysis.

5.
A Theory
of Organisational
Development

Many theories of organisational development* arise from the study of the behaviour of people in small groups. There are a number of reasons for this:

> organisational development is concerned with the study of the behaviour of *people* in organisations and people relate to subsidiary groups rather than the organisation as a whole

> it is impossible to study and comprehend large organisations as a whole because their complexity is too great

> the behaviour of people in small groups, being the most manageable aspect of organisational behaviour to observe, seems to provide models that help us to understand organisations as a whole

> in any case, few organisations permit examination by outsiders of the whole organisation though many do ask for help with key or difficult groups.

The implications of the theory presented in this paper are:

1. behaviour in organisations can be predicted in broad terms though not in detail
2. behaviour changes over time, therefore any theory of organisational development must take the passage of time as a major variable
3. while behaviour cannot be totally changed or prevented it can be reasonably well understood; this understanding provides a marginal but significant advantage in enabling managers to deal successfully with the behaviour that arises
4. if most management activity is a form of crisis management, a primary managerial skill is to understand the nature of crisis and how organisational crises occur and are resolved.

My basic theory is simple. It suggests that all organisations pass through a cycle of four phases in all parts of the system but that the phases do not coincide at any time for all parts of the organisation. Nevertheless, an organisation can be identified as being largely in one phase or another which is, therefore, over-ridingly characteristic. The

---

* Organisational development refers to the ways in which organisations develop. Organisation (sič) Development, or 'OD,' refers to the management techniques used to assist organisations and members to develop. See later chapter 6 on OD in Education.

major determinants of this general characteristic are both the leadership style of the senior member or leader and the stage in its development which the organisation has reached.

This basic theory has been described by Fink and others and is appended. Similarity to Tavistock theories based on the work of W. R. Bion will be apparent.

The theory suggests that organisations, and distinctive parts of organisations, develop cyclically through the four phases of:

DEPENDENCY
COUNTERDEPENDENCY
MUTUALITY
AUTONOMY

Passage is through these phases in the given order. Entry into each phase is dependent on the successful resolution of issues in the preceding phase. Phases cannot be omitted nor can the work necessary for conflict resolution be avoided. In fact, it may be that little can be done to accelerate the progression other than by helping the members to 'work through' the problems in each phase. An O.D. intervention would therefore be a means of helping the resolving of issues rather than preventing them or avoiding them.

Dependency

All organisations begin in a state of dependency. That is to say, every member is dependent on others, generally his superiors, and the phase is characterised by an unwillingness to take individual or group initiatives and responsibilities by claiming reliance on superiors or leaders. Overall, members of the organisation are dependent on the most senior manager or boss and require him to accept responsibility and make all major decisions. It does not follow that they will like or even approve of his decisions, simply that they are unwilling to depart from what they believe they *should* do. Of course, no manager can fulfil such expectations since he will inevitably wish to share some responsibilities and tasks. Subordinates will do as they are asked but with no personal commitment or identification. Though they may appear to be obedient (perhaps in order to secure favour) they make little investment in the organisation (whatever the protestations to the contrary); they wish essentially to be absolved of any responsibility. When things go wrong they can blame the boss because they took no part in the decision-making process even though the organisation may have set up a highly complex formal decision-sharing mechanism. In this phase, members require and need an autocrat at the head and always respond appropriately and obediently. This state of dependency occurs irrespective of the style of leadership of the boss and irrespective of any formal structures which are aimed at a different response. Autocratic and paternalistic bosses find this stage a reasonably agreeable one. Disagreement from subordinates only adds savour to the exercise of authority. But in fact members do not see the boss as he sees himself, anyway. Everyone has an irrational set of expectations and fantasies about the boss which are continuously augmented retrospectively ("I always thought a good boss would do such and such", said after he has done the contrary). Many of these expectations are quite unreasonable but are still firmly held – thus a boss with a declared science background is expected also to be an authority on artistic and creative matters.

Given a benign environment outside the organisation, this phase of dependency may last for a long time. ('Benign' in this sense means non-threatening to the organisation). But few environments are benign and so the dysfunctional effects of dependency begin to proliferate. A major problem for many bosses is their inability to delegate fully responsibility for the execution of work but in this phase they are on a hiding to nothing whatever they do. If they really do delegate, subordinates refuse to accept the delegation yet if they don't delegate, subordinates demand that they do so. Additionally, much apparent rebellion is just a means of proving dependency – such as disagreeing with the boss but seeking his approval for the expression of disagreement.

Counterdependency

Counterdependency follows from a facing up to the fact of dependency. It is characterised by rebellion, truculence, diffidence, destructiveness alienation and ganging up both on the boss and other groups. There is still a basic need for dependency and any efforts by the management to return to dependency will be welcomed, because the new state is so uncomfortable. Most organisations survive by remaining in a state of retreat from counterdependency which is the "political condition"* and the reason why most organisations (especially non-commercial organisations like schools and colleges) are run on the basis of political behaviour (power blocks, influence groups, backstair agreements, vote collecting etc. etc.). There is a great deal of personal cruelty in this phase. Scapegoats are set up, reputations destroyed, fall-guys presented, front-men sacrificed and intriguers brutalised. The weak and innocent are always hurt first as they are presented to the boss for slaughter – an individual set up as a counter-leader to the boss who has to be destroyed in order that neither the boss nor the other

---

* e.g. involvement in trade union activity.

subordinates lose too much face, and to prevent progress into full counterdependency which everyone recognises as being too uncomfortable.

In most cases, counterdependency is resolved by sacking the boss (or a scapegoat) whereupon the organisation returns to a period of dependency on the new boss. In this period of long term crisis and disruption, the boss loses the support of his superiors, probably people outside the organisation who are very concerned with the public image. But none of the organisation's problems have been resolved and the process starts again. For counterdependency to be resolved satisfactorily, the membership/subordinates have to prove to themselves that they can manage without the boss. To do this they must actually dispense with him totally in the psychological sense. This is a major organisational crisis for the boss since he has to face the reality that the organisation *can* do without him. In experimental groups so far,* this abandoning of the boss has been achieved only when it was discovered by subordinates that the boss was in fact vulnerable; that he was not only human and frail but actually incompetent or ineffective. And the boss actually experienced this failure and desolation himself.

The explanation is perhaps obvious. Counterdependency is simply the reaction to dependency. Having discovered that they are not really independent of the boss, the subordinates try to force him into accepting responsibility for them, that is, to force him into dependency again. In so far as they rebel against him, their rebellion is dependent on him (since it is him they rebel against). To achieve real independence they have to act without him quite independently and *know* that they are in fact independent. If the boss did not also feel their independence, then there could be no real independence. So the psychological break must be complete for everyone. However, having actually achieved independence, there is no further need to continue rebellion and a sorting out of new relationships among the whole membership is necessary for entry into the next phase. The boss himself can be a partner in the establishing of new relationships and he is invited back into the organisation.

At this juncture a second crisis occurs. The members invite the boss back on their terms and the boss apparently accepts. However, he cannot accept on their terms because he still holds the position of boss in relation to the formal structure of the organisation and the world outside. Consequently, he reasserts his position and a battle ensues until an agreement (or accommodation) can be made in which the

---

* A series of experimental OD Groups at the Anglian Regional Management Centre 1975-78 provides the experimental evidence for these organisational phenomena.

needs of the subordinates and the needs of the boss are reconciled. The problem is now one of collective and designated authority. The boss retains certain areas of authority and these have to be reconciled with the organisational need for authority to be shared. If reconciliation can be agreed, the organisation can move into a period of mutuality.

During Dependency and Counterdependency, a number of behaviours occur which are employed to avoid facing the real but deep and frightening issues that face the group or organisation. Organisationally the most significant is a preoccupation with order and structure, in fact for its own sake and as a means of dealing with the disturbances and uncertainty in the organisation which is seen as a move into chaos. People deal with uncertainty by seeking new structures, setting up committees and working parties, holding meetings, presenting reports and generally trying to make the intangible appear more certain. Bosses themselves are often a party to this process because they are themselves uncertain about the real issues in the organisation. Setting up structures is an attempt to exert control but since structures properly *follow upon* reality, no structures can be imposed without the deeper reality being known (and hence can never actually be 'imposed', they can only emerge). Furthermore, since all organisations are dynamic, structures themselves must evolve and change; to reassert traditional or conventional structures will inevitably lead to conflicts.

A second feature is the throwing up and testing out of new leaders and leadership 'structures'. On the basis of Bion's theory of groups, there will be groups that bid for leadership, groups that make alliances (whatever their inherent incompatabilities) for their own ends against other groups and the boss, and groups that escape from the conflict either by pretending it does not really exist or that they can manage without the rest of the organisation. (Of course, some groups within the organisation may have already developed themselves beyond rebellion but insofar as they relate to the larger organisation, their behaviour is parallel to that of other groups). Another characteristic is the need for "completeness" or "universality". Decisions are called for which have complete and total agreement among all the members of the organisation. When votes are called for it is demanded that majority decisions (even of 1 vote) are upheld by everyone. Deviance cannot be tolerated nor can differences of action/behaviour or even opinion. Much effort is put into the political activities concerned with achieving power, agreement and controlled behaviour. A typical behaviour sequence, concerned with the avoidance of facing up to conflicts and disagreement, is for fragmentation to occur whereby no one will take any initiative at all but for there to be a high rate of activity in small groups; then there is a general feeling of unease in which activity almost stops—

a waiting period; next is the public expression of anxiety followed by attempts to resolve the 'problem' by structural methods — that is, by some expression of unanimity or general agreement. If this unity is openly denied, the possibility of finding the conflict and resolving it becomes possible because the situation is now open to admitting and facing up to conflict. But most organisations shy away from even admitting the existence of basic and significant conflict.

When the boss adopts a high profile and an interventionist approach, progress will be impeded and overall behaviour will be regressive. The answer seems to be for the boss to take a low profile, to avoid taking initiatives but to be aware of the inevitable progress of events so that he can survive the process. He can do this by concerning himself with protecting the organisation from outside interference but letting events within take their natural course. In practice, he will be able to gain natural allies from within the organisation if he himself is familiar with organisational development theory and practice, has a reference group of O.D. experts as personal counsellors and has been trained in group counselling. Without such personal support it seems unlikely that any boss can both understand what is happening in his organisation and act appropriately. The alternative would appear to be a form of political behaviour in a political condition as described earlier.

Mutuality or Interdependence

In this phase, the problem of the boss's authority has been largely resolved. Groups and individuals function interdependently and there is a strong sense of organisational ethos, with well understood norms of behaviour and generally accepted values. It is a fairly comfortable phase but not especially creative since deviance is the great fear. However, most organisations would have done pretty well to reach a situation in which people could really communicate with one another and where the over-riding wish is to help rather than interfere. Many bosses will not find this phase particularly challenging because they do not have a dominant role within the organisation and will need to go outside to achieve the many personal satisfactions deriving from power, influence, prestige and significance.

Mutuality becomes a form of dependence which must be dealt with by the same processes of rebellion that characterised counter-dependency. Probably this process will be less upsetting to individuals since groups are involved, but the most creative members of the organisation will be fighting for their individuality. Eccentrics and odd-balls will have a bad time as the better socialised members move towards autonomy. But there will be much resistance to change and many of the old familiar behaviours will recur.

There are often false instances of mutuality in the earlier phases of development. These are generally attempts to avoid conflict by denial — "We are a happy organisation and we all understand one another — go away and do not disturb our happiness". Mutuality is a common fantasy in organisations unable to face and deal with their problems. True mutuality (not pairing) has to be won and can only come after the traumas of rebellion. In any case, mutuality will not suit everyone and so this third phase of organisation development may not be so easy as many may hope for.

Autonomy

This is an ideal state of personal independence and interdependence among members and groups where individuality is valued and supported. Most organisations experience periods of autonomy when they are at their most creative but it must be doubtful if "automony" is compatable with 'organisation', in the formally established or institutional sense. For there to be a real climate of autonomy in an organisation, status differentials have to be of little consequence but most organisations offer promotion and salary increases as essential aspects of functioning. Since few organisations are the sole example of their kind but have parallel organisations competing for members from the same resource pool, one organisation cannot stand out against the others. However, departments within an organisation may move towards autonomy and the larger organisation can learn to deal with differences within itself. Certainly, near autonomy is possible within organisational peer groups like a management committee or governing/managing board and within teams.

An Organisation Development Strategy

The question arises as to whether an organisation can be helped to pass through these phases of development. According to the theory, the development is inevitable, occurs in its own time, is temporarily reversible but in the long term inexorable. What kind of intervention is possible, and by whom, to ease this development? Some indication has already been given with regard to the boss and the boss is the most significant figure. It must be recognised that the boss is as integral a part of the development process as any other member; indeed he is the most critical. Unless he is part of the intervention, there can be no progress. Hence, it seems essential that he be trained in understanding the theory and also in the counselling/consulting techniques which are necessary to weather the storms of the organisation. Such training is 'experiential' by means of Organisation Development groups which are a form of T-Group in which the members are enabled to experience the behavioral

71

phenomena of the developmental process. With this training the boss is in a strong position to understand what is happening in his organisation and how to help the process constructively. Additionally he needs personal support of a reference group that ideally remains totally unconnected with the organisation. This group is his personal support when the outside authorities threaten him as head of the organisation during the second, rebellious, stage.

The training that the boss has should be shared by as many people in the organisation as possible, but certainly key position holders. Probably some form of simple T-Group on an NTL/Leeds model rather than a Tavistock model would be best; a counselling approach being used by the 'trainer'. These groups should be on a section or departmental basis because the section/department is a key unit in Organisation Development. Each department will develop separately and differently and the managerial task of intergration concerns departments rather than individuals. In practice, not all departments/sections will agree to this group work so only the willing groups should be trained initially. It is, however, essential for the senior management group to work with a counsellor/consultant for the whole period of the intervention which may last several years.

In this intervention, the work of the consultant counsellors is confined to group work and does not extend to the daily normal work of the organisation. The reason for this is that the members of the organisation must work out their own problems among themselves. In any case, consultants cannot deal with the organisation as a whole. The expectation is that the learning in small groups will transfer to other groups and larger groups. Of course, for many people this transference will not take place because behaviour modification cannot be made on such a grand scale but the more creative members of the organisation *will* learn and their behaviour will be effective, and it is this that really matters. The job of the consultants is to give support and help not to create their own organisation. As the intervention takes effect, structural and administrative problems will be solved by the members themselves in a dynamic way and there is no need at all for the consultants to concern themselves directly with such matters even though these are the issues for which the organisation will first call them in.

Phases of Organizational Crisis

Phase	Inter-Personal Relations	Inter Group Relations	Communi-cation	Leadership and decision Making	Problem Handling	Planning and Gaol Setting	Structure
Shock (Dependency)	Fragmented	Disconnected	Random	Paralyzed	None	Dormant	Chaotic
Defensive Retreat (counter Dependency)	Protective Cohesion	Alienated	Ritualized	Autocratic	Mechanistic	Expedient	Traditional
Acknowl-edgement (Mutuality)	Confrontation (supportive)	Mutuality	Searching	Participative	Explorative	Synthesizing	Experi-menting
Adaptation and Change (Autonomy)	Interdepend-ent	Coordinated	Authentic Congruent	Task-Centered	Flexible	Exhaustive and Integrative	Organic

TIME ——————→

*From Stephen L. Fink. et al. J. of Applied Behavioural Science. Vol. 7 No. 1. 1971.

6.
Organisation Development in Education

Organisation Development, or 'O.D.' in its generally abbreviated form, is a familiar term in management training and consultancy. Though practically unknown in Education in the United Kingdom, 'O.D.' is not uncommon in North America and we are likely to hear more of the term especially as attention is drawn to the techniques required for the management of innovation and the implementation of new curricular concepts.

The term itself is too broad to carry precise meaning and in general usage it covers a variety of different approaches to the management of change and innovation. Since there is no proprietorship of the term, there would appear to be no means of circumscribing the meaning and we shall have to live with a term that comes to mean quite different things to different people. The historical origins of the term are in the work in group dynamics of the Tavistock Institute in the U.K. and the National Training Laboratories* in the U.S.A. The core activity of 'pure' O.D. is the T-Group (Training Group) which is a means of helping individuals to understand the behaviour of people in groups and also their own behaviour as group members. There is a fairly wide variety of types of T-Groups, T-Group methods of training, trainer styles and T-Group uses as well as major differences between the Tavistock approach and the N.T.L. approach.

The previous paragraph may sound esoteric in terminology but it is important to understand that 'O.D.' arises from the development of group dynamics training, is somewhat specialised and has developed in certain specific directions while similar management activities have a different origin and are not properly Organisation Development. This confusion over the real nature of O.D. is one of the problems for O.D. workers at the present time. Thus many activities in education that are called 'O.D.' cannot be in the real tradition of O.D. because they are too brief in duration and do not derive from group dynamics in the Training Group sense.†

T-Group training is concerned with the problems of leadership, decision-making, problem solving, interpersonal relation and the presentation of self in an organisational context. In a T-Group the

---

* Books representative of group training by the Tavistock Institute and National Training Labotatories are:
  Rice, A. K., *Learning for Leadership*, Tavistock, London 1968, and Bradford, L. P., Gibb, J. R. & Benne, K. D. (Eds) *T-Group Theory & Laboratory Method*, John Wiley, New York 1964.
† Miles, Matthew B., *Learning to Work in Groups*, Teachers College Columbia 1971. is a simplification and adaptation of group training methods and is a useful guide to conducting meetings and conferences.

members have the task of examining their own behaviour as it occurs with the help of a 'trainer' or 'facilitator'. The trainer will himself behave according to a pattern somewhere on the continuum from initial non-participation to that of Rogerian counselling. (These two extremes may be characterised as 'Tavistock' and 'Rogerian'*). One or other form of T-Group is used within the organisation to help members to a greater insight into their own and colleagues' behaviour. The T-Groups as frequently used in management training involve members who start as strangers to one another, but they are also an essential part of O.D. 'interventions' where the participants will have worked together in the same department or at least in the same organisation. An O.D. practitioner, or consultant, will employ his T-Group trainer skills in his job as consultant to the organisation or department.

Not unnaturally, from the "non-directive," free flowing training groups, there has grown a need for systematic packages – exercises, games, activities, questionnaires – which became the tangible elements in the repertoire of skills used by many O.D. practitioner in the same way that psychiatrists, counsellors, consultants employ devices or exercises to help matters along. These activities have been passed from one practitioner to another and several collections published – such as the NASA Space Shot, the Zero-sum Game, the Johari Window, Blakes Grid.† They are means of helping the group members to concentrate on a particular aspect of their behaviour. These exercises and games have become widely known in management training and are used quite legitimately by all sorts of people interested in group relations training. Some consultants have developed quite complicated 'packages' which are used in management training. But strictly speaking, their use alone does not constitute O.D.

Furthermore, while O.D. is concerned with helping organisations to change, it is so concerned in a specialised and limited way. Not all attempts to bring about change in an organisation are O.D. interventions; O.D. is not synonymous with the management of change. An event of structured exercises even over several days is not an O.D. event because the essence of O.D. practitioner behaviour is coping with the unpredictable, the unexpected and the undiscovered. No highly structured programme with clearly defined objectives can be an O.D.

---

* See Rogers, Carl. Encounter Groups Penguin 1973.

† The best collection of games and exercises is in the series, *Handbook of Structured Experiences for Human Relations Training* Edited by Pfeiffer J. William & Jones, John E. issued in an annual volume since 1969 and published by University Associates Press, Iowa.

event because such determinism is incompatible with O.D. values. Yet many structured programmes are provided under the title of 'O.D.' when in the strict sense they are training programmes of a different kind.*

The distinction may be clearer if we understand that O.D. is concerned with helping people to understand how and why people behave in groups as they do, and is not primarily concerned with the nature of the change. The concern is with the 'process' of change rather than the product, since our desire for the product is an expression of personal values which the O.D. practitioner may not share. Most normal management interventions are concerned with helping members of an organisation to bring about a desired change, which generally speaking the consultant shares. However, in the O.D. intervention the practitioner or consultant cannot know what the best outcome will be hence his concern is with the processes by which the group or organisation members achieve agreement on what they believe to be right for them at the time.

Of course, O.D. consultants have their own set of values and try to be quite clear about their own personal values and those of O.D. practitioners in general. Most O.D. practitioners will have some association with the various national O.D. Networks (which publish directories of members and their interests), and in the U.K. also the Group Relations Training Association and/or the Association of Teachers of Management. There is a distinct culture among O.D. practitioners and consultants, most of whom would refer to themselves as Applied Behavioural Scientists and who tend to be 'humanistic psychologists' in some way or another. O.D. practitioners as a profession do not belong to a formal association or professional body but by the nature of their work they tend to meet together informally.

Among the values that O.D. practitioners share are a belief in organisational democracy; the development of trust among members of the group; openness and sharing of ideas, values and reactions among colleagues; emotional honesty or facing up to one's feelings; self-respect and respect for the autonomy of others with whom one works; and belief in the possiblity of continual learning and self-development.†
While these may seem to be 'soft' values, most O.D. practitioners would adopt a very hard line to achieve them within an organisation where they were employed as consultant for without exception, organisations

---

* In many ways, the 'classic' work on O.D. in schools falls under these strictures — Schmuck, Richard A. & Runkel, P. J. *Second Handbook of Organisation Development in Schools,* University of Oregon Press, 1977.

† This list is based on a paper produced in February 1975 by an O.D. Group, members of the Association of Teachers of Management.

resist these humanistic (or Christian) values seeing them being irrelevant to the reality of their ongoing practical tasks.

There are three basic assumptions on which all O.D. interventions work. These are firstly a belief in the validity of experiential learning as the only way individuals can be helped to understand their own behaviour and that of others in the organisational (group) setting. Secondly, that all behaviour in formal organisations represents a manifestation of underlying problems and conflicts which constitute the hidden agenda. Thirdly, that the 'presenting' problem can only be solved when the underlying problems have been identified and resolved. Because organisations resist the uncovering of causes that these three principles require, the main work of the practitioner is concerned with trying to break through resistances. For this reason, most organisations, heads and members, tend to be unwilling for thoroughgoing O.D. interventions to take place. Most commonly senior members invite O.D. interventions but require to be excluded themselves and for their subordinates only to be subjected to the O.D. event. It follows, that the major problem for O.D. consultants is to gain entry to the organisation and for the organisation to commit itself to a lengthy and painful process of self-examination.

O.D. interventions are particularly consuming of time and commitment. It is doubtful if any organisation could benifit from an O.D. programme of anything less than twelve months, once entry by the consultant has been agreed. It is more realistic, even in school terms, to think of from three to five years. And before the programme starts, several months (even a year) of negotiation can be expected since the consultant's first task is to achieve personal acceptability from the majority of the staff. Once the programme has begun, the consultantants start a process of sensing out problems, bring parties and individuals together to resolve conflicts and misunderstandings, attempt the resolving of issues, give personal counselling to members with role and personal problems, help the organisation to develop new and realistic structures and procedures. Basically, because an O.D. axiom is that all organisations are in a state of conflict,but that conflict resolution is the basis of creativity, the method of O.D. is to uncover unrecognised conflicts, help people to face up to them and work through them to resolution. This is a decidedly painful and often unwelcome process and some organisations terminate the process in mid-stream because the situation has become too uncomfortable.

Not unnaturally, O.D. practitioners, rather like psycho-analysts, tend to see the causes of problems in specific and particular terms. They see all organisational problems in terms of inter-personal relationships and tend to work on a number of consequent assumptions, such as that the senior manager is always a factor in the discontent of his subordinates, or that individuals can only change that part of a problem that is truly their own and cannot blame others for their discomfort.

An example will illustrate this. As an O.D. consultantant I was invited to help a secondary school with its problems of time-tabling. I had published a paper on school time-tabling* and this was my passport of creditability. I was invited to visit the school for two days to work with the Deputy Head and Senior Mistress on time-table construction. Both these members of the management team accepted the theoretical validity of my approach and some time was spent on the preliminary matrix for the timetable. However, it soon became apparent that the timetable itself was not the problem. Although the school was on a split-site, quite simple technical solutions were possible. But the timetable was not the basic problem, nor was the curriculum or even the matter of goals and objectives for the school. The problem areas that required attention were more difficult to face and resolve since they involved the self-esteem of the Head and his difficulties in delegating responsibility; and also questions of commitment, motivation and contract of several senior staff. In the time available, little more could be done by me as consultant than help the Head and Senior Mistress to face up to the existence of difficulties in their own personal relationship. Little more than a touching of the surface was possible and yet the whole situation called for several months of work to pass through the stages of facing up to the real problems, working through them, and creating a climate for creative and autonomous development.

In the example given, progress was remarkably rapid and the little achieved gave grounds for hope. In other situations, the senior member has felt himself to be too much under threat and has withdrawn, often at the point when a good opportunity for facing up and resolution had arisen. In these situations, the O.D. consultant is in a very open and fluid situation. The need is to sense out the situation and seize opportunities and this cannot be done according to a previously determined design; he must work "off the cuff", extemporising, testing out, taking informed risks and recovering from bad situations. Obviously, very special skills are required and very few people have received adequate training†.

---

* H. L. Gray: The Secondary School Timetable: A Matrix Approach. Anglian Regional Management Centre 1974.

† A Master's Degree in Organisation Development is offered at Sheffield Polytechnic and shorter courses are available at some other polytechnics and Colleges. There is also a Master's degree in Educational Management at Sheffield Polytechnic that has a high O.D. content while at Huddersfield Polytechnic there is an O.D. Unit in the Management Department and O.D. based short and award bearing courses inEducation. Most O.D. practitioners have training in psychology, social psychology, organisation studies or behavioural sciences.

Much of the work of an O.D. practitioner is intuitive – based on experience but risky since he is generally fumbling for solutions rather knowing the answers beforehand. In this respect O.D. work is a creative art – like the writer who knows the ideas will come but cannot know what they are until they arrive. Yet O.D. is no place for the inexperienced because other people will suffer from ineptitude.

While it is necessary to stress the fact that O.D. interventions are initially very uncomfortable for an organisation, given enough time and a skilled practitioner the effects are much more satisfying than other forms of management consultancy because the process of problem solving involves all those concerned in a totally personal way so that they develop complete ownership of the solutions to the problem situation and in the process clients themselves learn to practice the O.D. skills of personal relationships. Nevertheless, some senior managers are greatly threatened by O.D. solutions particularly if they are authoritarian personalities; are highly ambitious and identify personally with their organisation; or if they are disposed to behave 'politically' in order to pursue their career objectives. The moral values of O.D. practitioners may conflict with those who take a different view of organisational reality, and I am clear that O.D. is not the only or the best way to solve all organisational problems. On the other hand, O.D. values of respect for individuals, concern for individual recognition and achievement, looking for the best in people and discounting the worst, would seem to be compatible with our current educational values and it may be hoped that there will be a cautious increase in O.D. interventions in our educational institutions.

7.
The Organisational Significance of Teams in Educational Institutions

Education is saturated with teams. As soon as a new idea or project is conceived a team is set up to develop it. Th8s is especially true of academic courses and innovative ideas when team members set to work with a will producing discussion papers about philosophy, objectives and criteria of evaluation. Invariably social and psychological problems ensue which interrupt the work flow and often lead to reorganisation and sometimes to the complete re-forming of the team.

In spite of the widespread experience of dissatisfaction with the way very many educational teams work, there seems to be little evidence that many people have tried to change their ways and there is a trail of unsuccessful teams littering the history of all educational institutions. Surely someone has had time to reflect on what has happened and attempted a critique of team building, and the place of teams in organisational life? This paper is an attempt to contribute to a re-evaluation of how teams work and how they relate to their parent organisation.

To begin with, I am acutely aware that for me there has been a gap between the commonly held theoretical stance in training courses on team building, and involvement in actual teams in real institutions. I have had considerable experience of training situations where I have used Applied Behavioural Science* approaches to team building. But in the early years of my work they depended more heavily on other people's theory rather than my own experience. Training situations usually consist of groups of people who do *not* share membership of the same work team but who come specially for a programme in team building where trainers use a variety of exercises, and processes‡. Many of my early programme/courses were concerned with teaching people the principles of social organisation relevent to working in teams and while it is known that course members did attempt to apply their learning in the back home situation it has been impossible to observe a systematic attempt at team building from scratch using behavioural principles

---

* The term 'Applied Behavioural Science' may by unfamiliar to many U.K. readers and appear cumbersome. It refers to an approach to social psychology based on the study of the dynamics of group behaviour and is used instead of other terms (such as social-psychological) because its reference is more precise.

† See, for example:
Gray, H. L. and Cunningham, I. *Management Courses for Teachers* in Br. Journal of In-Service Education, Vol. 1 No. 1 Autumn 1974.
Gray, H. L. *Training in the Management of Education:*
    An Experiential Approach
in Educational Administration, Vol. 1 No. 1 1972.
Gray, H. L. *Understanding Organisations: A Clinical Approach*
    Br. Journal of In-Service Education Vol. 0 Spring 1976.

within an organisation where the problems of team building are consciously under observation.

More recently, however, I have had the opportunity to become involved in the creation of new teams and this paper is a reflection on those experiences. I am, however, aware that I am generalising from my perceptions of the effect of team building on the parent organisations but in fact believe it worthwhile to attempt some hypotheses about the significance of teams in organisations.

All new teams work under some pressure. Since they are set up in an organisational context they are subject to pressure from the parent organisation – perceived, imaginary and real. A real pressure is some deadline such as the date of commencement of a new course, a CNAA submission or the material demands of members' jobs elsewhere in the organisation. An imaginary pressure (which may be described as a fantasy) is a belief that there are certain deadlines or institutional requirements, but this 'reality' is untested and the pressures turn out on examination to be either different or non-existent. I would define a perceived pressure as an assumption such as a ground-rule or an expectation that the members accept as axiomatic for them – though no one else may have the same perception. An example would be the assumption that course content should not overlap with the work of another team. Pressures may be shared or personal to one individual.

Organisations are inclined to have certain expectations of teams, such as that they should make "positive" decisions, achieve a "tangible" product or "quantity" of output, and have an indentifiable, defined and cohesive membership. (In the context of this paper the 'organisation' means other members of the organisation since organisations do not have disembodied expectations.) Key individuals, such as members in executive positions, tend to employ these expectations evaluatively so that a working party that does not "produce" a course is seen as being less effective than one that presents, say, 50 pages of a course programme.

Among the first tasks of most teams is the electing of, or accepting the appointment of, a team leader or convenor. Some teams formalise themselves even more by appointing a chairman and secretary or recorder.The team then attempts to define its task in terms of objectives– a process which involves a discussion of the "philosophy" of the task. This is particularly so if it is a course development team. These two groups of assumptions – about chairman/leadership and about procedure – in practice beg the question – since all teams get lost in questions of leadership and procedure by making the erroneous assumption that they can either be taken as given or are capable of resolution before the work of the team begins. In reality, leadership always remains a matter at issue – as explained below – while objectives and philosophy are discovered as a consequence of the work of the team rather than as a prior condition.

Experience of research on teams suggests that leadership is always an open or unresolved issue because leadership is a function of the group process – i.e. of the way in which the team works on discovering its tasks or the value of the tasks it can most usefully work on. The more uncertainty over the nature of the task (e.g. a new course) and the more the team is concerned with exploring new ideas, the more leadership is a shared function. On the other hand, the clearer the task presented to the team, the more effective will it be for one person to accept responsibility if the organisational demands are to be satisfied. Comparatively few group tasks in creative* situations are most easily facilitated by a single leader. The issue is over the commitment of the leader, as a control influence, to his interpretation of the task. For example, if the leader believes a course in urban geography should exclude village life his efforts will be directed towards achieving agreement on his interpretation.

Rather than teams starting off with a leader committed to the task of the group – that is, a task to which he has some form of commitment and interpretation – there should be an independent arbiter or facilitator whose only job is to help the group to do its work; he himself will be free of commitment to the task, and committed only to facilitating the team work. Such a situation, however, moves the team well away from control by the organisation and may well lead to autonomous behaviour in which the team functions almost independently of the parent organisation.

The problem of setting objectives is that objectives can only arise out of a common experience. A team cannot have task objectives or even agreement on philosophy until the task is completed. Objectives and philosophy can only derive from a clear understanding of what things are about. Few, if any, teams know before they start what they are going to achieve and this is as true for academic course programmes as of future-planning exercises. Early discussion of objectives and philosophy is an avoidance of the relevant task because they cannot be settled until it has been discovered how the team members need to function together. No team can know what it wants to do until it has become a psychologically close group. All my experience of teams suggests that deciding on aims and objectives and discussing policy is simply one

---

* A creative situation is simply one in which there are no routine or preordained solutions. Perhaps newer situations are like this but few 'organisations' so perceive it.

way of expressing conflict and disagreement at cerebral level without resolving the basic emotional conflicts. As individuals present "philosophy" papers or statements of objectives they are playing with their terms of entry into the group but trying to depersonalise the conflict which is potential in differing attitudes and standpoints. As certain philosophical standpoints win the day as a consequence of power-coercive behaviour, so members are drawn into alliances with, or alienation from, the other group members. Many groups fail because conflict is disguised as discussion at the intellectual level rather than worked through as experience at the emotional level. Yet emotional accord is the prior condition for working intellectual issues.

Social psychologists are accustomed to referring to the activity of a group as having two aspects — the aspect of task and the aspect of process. In psychological terms the actual task may not be (indeed rarely is) the same as the expressed or overt task. A team concerned with a programme in economic geography will have a number of 'tasks' to complete which are concerned with needs and relationships among members and which have to be resolved or completed before the programme overtly described as "economic geography" can be dealt with. The manner in which these activities are performed is part of the process activity. Unless a team works through the process appropriate to its own unique situation which in turn arises out of its personal composition, it will be unable to complete any collective tasks satisfactorily.

The important point to remember is that the psychological relationships between members of a team are the first concern of team building. Unless (creative) psychological bonding occurs, the team cannot satisfactorily give its attention to the overt task. Psychological bonding is the exchange or bargaining relationship by which each member commits himself to a continued association with the other team members.

Creative team membership arises when each individual perceives the team as offering him satisfactory returns (i.e. exchanges) for his contributions and when he seeks to prolong the association. Creativity results from a willingness to stay in the team and to work on differences with other members so that a satisfactory resolution occurs. As the relationship among members develops, certain norms and givens are developed (assumptions, axioms of belief and behaviour) and these provide a value basis for activity. Hence the group members come to share a critical number of 'values' with a consequence that conflicts are worked through in terms of these values. Out of a system of common values arise common objectives. These objectives are derived from values; they do not exist either *a priori* or in their own right. Of course, all objectives derive from values and it is surprising that so much curriculum work has been preoccupied with setting objectives rather than the basic question of different personal values among members.

Teams exist in an organisational context to serve the purposes of the organisation and also the purposes of members. Purposes may be expressed in terms of the needs members have; and these are quite personal. It is most unlikely that anyone can be personally committed to the tasks of a team, *per se* except as a means of satisfying his own psychological needs – such as affiliation, achievement and power. It is reasonable to assume that no one is completely disinterested in what happens and that altruism is dependent on self-satisfaction, anything else achieved being a bonus. It is important to understand this because some members claim organisational concern or personal disinterest as a means of gaining (personal) control.

Teams within institutions exist within a power-control environment. The organisation brings pressures of control which can be both supportive and disruptive. Members of the team may use the parent organisation as a source of sanctions as well as resources. A team will be in a state of functional equilibrium when all members use the parent organisation only for generally supportive resources and not for personalised sanctions. But individuals who find themselves excluded from the team will be tempted to use institutional sanctions to support their own position and to counter the effectiveness of others. For the institution, functional equilibrium exists only when teams make minimum demands on the parent organisation but give maximum returns. An individual using institutional sanctions uses resources from the parent organisation and by alienating team members prevents the required return to the institution. High ranking members of the institution often identify closely in a personal way with the organisation (i.e. they impute their personal objectives and needs to the impersonal organisation). Hence they often perceive the hauling back of the team into line as a victory for control and good management whereas in practice it is rather the contrary because the organisation has been weakened by alienation and decreased commitment. Renegades from a team are likely to receive support from superiors because they offer an opportunity for control to return to the parent organisation. Defaulters always gain the ear of organisational superiors.

Team membership and attendance always fluctuates so that team membership is not static in any sense. In fact, a fluctuating attendance is an important positive factor in team building for two reasons. The return of an absent member is an occasion for restating the position of the group and of incorporating the returned member's views and experience. A test of strength and solidarity is measured by the ability of the group to cope with absences and re-entry. Furthermore, fluctuating membership and attendance keeps the team open to influences from outside—from the parent organisation and also the larger social system. Openness to influence is a strong positive factor in group health. A continuing group is an arena for continuous bargaining: bargaining is the process by which individuals make their contracts with each other. A prior condition for the making of a contract is the process of negotiating entry or "buying in".* This bargaining is never completed but for each individual there is a point when he considers himself to have 'joined' the team though he may not be aware of this until after he has made the critical psychological contract. Since the process is one of open negotiation, the role of a designated, appointed or elected chairperson or leader is critical since it embodies the major contracting party. The external designating of leaders creates a situation in which bargaining cannot be free but can only be with the institution the designated leader represents. Strong traditional leadership impedes the process of negotiation and is always potentially dysfunctional.

Two methods for avoiding the leadership hassles are to have a process consultant or facilitator and/or for all group members to have trained together in a T-Group or Encounter Group. Group members previously trained in Encuonter use a co-counselling mode of working in which problems of internal status are 'worked through' and continuing external relationships determined as the group members perceive it and agree. Such a team will be leaderless (i.e. have shared leadership) internally though the acceptance of formalised external links will be understood; activated according to circumstances. 'Leaderless' teams are very disturbing to other members of the parent organisation because they are administratively untidy. Administrators do not value either creativity or effectiveness as such but do value lines of supposed communication and normative formalisation. The administrator and the commander prefer pigeon holes to people; simple accepting response in preference to dialogue. But these external expectations have nothing to do with team building; to consider them as requirements of team building is to confuse the three issues of multiple expectations, real communication and the true function of the team in the institution.

The important psychological contracts for each team member are with the other team members. Sometimes the contracts made within the

---

* This concept has been developed in its organisational application in H. L. Gray, *Exchange and Conflict in the School*, in Houghton, V. *et al*. Management in Education Ward Lock/Open University 1976.

team are imcompatible with the contracts made with the organisation (by individuals and by the team as a whole). When this occurs it is an indication that the broader contractual situation between members and the organisation is unsatisfactory; members are unable to satisfy their needs in the larger organisation and have found creative outlets in the team. This is potentially a highly creative situation but most organisations lose the advantage and coerce the team into conformity by claiming the greater good or greater need of the organisation. Yet how can there be a greater good when it is at the expense of a creative and member group? For had the group not been a growth-point the group would have collapsed or been in close accord with the organisation. Such situations occur when one programme team comes up with a programme that is not in line with other teams. The sensible response is to allow the team to continue its developments in a somewhat different context. But the threat of creativity is usually so great that the team is disbanded by those it threatens who enlist the support of the administrative system with its preference for simplistic alignments.

Organisations can only benefit from these constituent teams if there is an understanding of how to use dissidence as a creative and not destructive force. This will only be possible when all members recognise that their view of the organisation is entirely personal and subjective and can only be identical with those of the organisation as the result of coercion. In the long run coercion is always dysfunctional and alienative. Inspite of the problem of relationships between a team and the parent organisation, the task of building the team must go on in its own right. Only when the team members have a feeling of belonging to the team can the creative process of linking the team into the organisation be attended to. To attempt the linking too early is to weaken completely the value of a strong team in the organisation. It is by developing strong semi-autonomous teams that the parent organisation copes with change because each team represents a strong link with the world outside as well as autonomous security within.* There is no way whereby organisational control can bring about strength to cope with change because the greater the control centred in the fewer hands, the more restricted will be the perspective on future development. Whenever sudden change occurs as the result of one or two individuals being in control that change is ineffective in direct relationships to the coercion involved, though in practice the worst

---

* The importance of teams as autonomous units is given theoretical support in the concept of 'loose coupling'.
See Karl E. Weick, "Educational Organisations as loosely Coupled Systems" in administrative Science Quarterly, March 1976, Vol. 21.

effect is generally mitigated by the presence of some residual energy for change. Heads of organisations need to be cautious about how much actual change is the consequence of their own actions.

In order for a team to fulfil its organisational function satisfactorily it must develop a high degree of autonomy of the parent institution before linking back into inter-dependence. As we have discussed already, institutions find great difficulty in permitting this process because it creates a threat to those in superior positions. There would appear to be some relationship between position in the formal hierarchy and vulnerability to threat from elsewhere. Threat occurs when there is explicit deviation from the institutionalised member's perception of how things ought to be — non-explicit deviation does not manifest a threat. Team members who see their loyalty or interests linked to institutional approval will be in conflict within themselves as well as with other team members and may find themselves unable to 'buy in' to the team at all. Subsequently they may justify and reinforce their opting out by using the organisation's view of the team to punish team members or coerce them into different terms of acceptance. Alternatively, team-building may be used by team members as a means of consolidating their withdrawal from or independence of the organisation. But they would still represent a loss to the organisation and it is an organisational weakness to allow the withdrawal to become complete without drawing back the energies concerned.

Organisations† tend to take a short term view of needs and objectives; that is, they assume that 'institutional' objectives over-ride individual and team needs and discover quantitive reasons why this is so. The fact is that short term satisfactions lead to long term dis-satisfactions as the history of higher educational institutions all to clearly shows. The problem of the teacher training institutions was that they always went for short-term solutions and it appears that the new institutes of Higher Education may be doing likewise—for instance, in their race for CNAA recognised courses. (The quantitive pressure, of course, is the availability of money in the form of student fees for recognised courses. But then the DES is not noted for its long term competence either.)

I stated earlier that a primary condition for team building was a sharing of values. In the context of the parent organisation these values may be at odds with those of the institution. Examples might be operational equality of status for members; a common view about the nature of education; openness and levelling; a perference for affective

---

† That is Senior and Middle range managers, as heads of organisations may take a broader view.

learning as against cognitive; a desire to use experiential modes rather than didactic. Such values will be accentuated as the team builds and polarisation against the parent institution is inevitable as the group members seek security in seperate identity. There seems little likelihood of a team continuing in existence without its own distinctive culture developing; the development of a separate culture is a basic characteristic of all teams as can be seen when we examine sports teams and student societies. In this regard deviance from the norms of the parent organisation is a characteristic of normal development.

Some of those willing to join a team may be seeking refuge from an uncomfortable position elsewhere in the organisation. All the members of the team, of course, may be doing this but for a few the team as a refuge may be more important than membership of the team as such. Such individuals will be prepared to accept membership on almost any terms but their commitment will be minimal. They will have problems of identity and identification, made worse by their discomfort also in the parent body. To the committed team members they represent a threat, both actively and passively, and a lot of energy will be used in exploring the situation at the expense of work on the collective tasks of the team. Usually such members are passengers, but in a real team building situation, (where members *work* at being a team), commitment or 'buying in' is a major issue. Instead of dealing with commitment late on in the life of the team when it is believed agreement has been reached, the issue is a prior condition of work. Unless there is 'buying in' there can be no work. Better not to start than to fall apart when everyone thinks the work has been concluded.

As a team builds and members come to share more and more values and objectives, and increasingly learn to cope with and accept differences among themselves, the need for a leader position decreases until the idea of a nominal leader is an irrelevance to the work of the group. The parent organisation may have no knowledge of how the team works and may require the team to nominate a leader. Generally such a demand presents little problem and is understood as a gesture but since nominated leadership is irrelevant to the team, the members may in public behave as if leadership is irrelevant or at least a shared function. Other members of the organisation may be disconcerted by this abrogation of responsibility and attempt coercion, but this will only increase the resistance of the team members to conformity. Interference may seem in order on the part of the parent organisation but it is seen as offensive to team members because (a) it is intrusion on their autonomy, (b) it is an expression of distrust of the members to organise themselves properly, (c) it is coercive and normative and (d) it relates to institutional fantasies and not team realities. (That is, the team *does*

93

work without a 'leader' and the organisation does *not* need a single point of relationship.) It must be recalled that creativity cannot occur within institutional procedures only in terms of deviance from them. Hence most organisations are endemically incapable of creativity and change in terms of their own administrative structures; they must learn to look to areas of deviance, non-conformity or exception for indications of change potential.

In many ways the qualities that go for the making of good teams are inconsistent with their being member units of a tightly organised system. Most institutions tend towards tight control — autocracy and bureaucracy — characteristics which are distinctive in rapidly changing situations and probably also in periods of consolidation, (since consolidation is a form of change and change adaptation) and quiescence (since quiescence is merely a lull before change pressures arise again). The problem for educational institutions at the present time is that they behave as if the present period were one of coping with changes that have yet to come. Polytechnics in a period of little or no growth find it very difficult to re-arrange any activity and the balance of activities. Everyone holds onto what he has got and administrative restraints increase considerably. In fact, during a period of standstill there should be more change and development, not less for much of it can occur in unconventional ways — to the consternation of the administration and senior academics. Almost everything that is currently being done in Higher Education is therefore inappropriate for the future. One solution may lie in the building of quasi-autonomous work teams in loose association rather than as tightly controlled sub-units of an administrative system. The question that might be asked of, for instance, course teams is what will happen when CNAA ceases to be a bargaining arena among the institutions? And what kind of education will be offered once student needs and not student numbers become the issue of the day?

8.
The Amalgamation of Institutions – Changing Educational Institutions

The amalgamation of institutions has been a common feature of recent public and private enterprise. Often the amalgamations have been somewhat hurried affairs and there has been little time for careful consideration of the implications. More seriously the method of amalgamation has most usually been based upon uninformed opinion rather than experience because there has been no coherent theory of organisations and organisational change to draw on. That many of the new institutions have had serious management problems is no surprise and some attempt should now be made to learn from what has happened and to build models of organisations and organisational behaviour that may be of help to those who contemplate further amalgamations. New theories do not have to be 'correct' but they should serve the function of providing a rational starting point for consideration and so go someway to preventing an occurrence of past disasters.

As a starting point for organisation theory a distinction must be made between the technological aspects of an organisation and the human aspects. Though the two inter-relate, it is important to understand how they relate. The technology of an organisation is the complex of mechanical processes which *must* be performed if the organisation is to function. The essential mechanical processes are often obscured by accretions which members have added out of preference but which are not essential. Part of the analysis of mechanical processes is concerned with distinguishing between the essential and the added processes. The more highly technological the organisational base, the easier to make the separation — as with chemical process companies. But many organisations do not depend on an essential technical process (for example banks, insurance companies, hospitals and schools) and in these cases it is often very difficult to distinguish technological process from human processes. For instance, the essential concept of "school" does not require a specific, universal technology, while the manufacture of nitric acid requires a largely specific technology.

The technological aspects of an organisation are 'inert'; that is to say, they do not of themselves change. Where they do change, the change is a consequence of human decision. All decisions are choices and all choices are preferred alternatives — preference being a human and personal quality and hence not universally valid or shared. All decisions in organisations are the result of preference and choice and we shall later discuss how they come about, but for the moment it must be understood that the essential human aspects of all organisations are arbitrary. Hence all organisations always have more choices open to them than they exercise. For the most part, the technical aspects of technology are a specialist sphere of knowledge. In addition to

97

technological knowledge is the "knowledge" of experience or opinion which makes up management theory. Management theory is the rationale for managerial behaviour and is entirely subjective in that it belongs to the individual who exercises managerial behaviour. Organisation theory, however, is the attempt to generalise on principles that are believed to be applicable to understanding how organisations function. It, too, may be subjective but is concerned with a different level of applicability from managerial pragmatism.

We have made two important distinctions. One is between the essential technology or mechanical processes of an organisation and the human behaviour which characterises the people who are members of organisations. The other is between management theory which is personal and prescriptive and organisation theory which is descriptive and predictive. Additionally, when we speak of organisations we almost always mean the behaviour of people in organisations (companies, firms, enterprises, institutions or whatever). To speak of an organisation is generally to speak of the people who are members of that organisation; only very seldom are we concerned with the mechanical technology.

Amalgamations may be between organisations with the same or similar technologies or between ones with different technologies. However, differences in mechanical technology are not a major issue. The substantive issue is concerned with the differences in culture between the two organisations. And culture is the pattern of values, norms and behaviours which characterise an identified group or organisation. In education the term 'ethos' is sometimes used loosely in this sense. No two schools can as seperate organisations, share the same ethos because part of that ethos is their separate identity — by definition.

Educational institutions have no essential technology though they may have a derivative technology. The essential educational process is the relationship between two or more people and institutionalisation is thereafter a matter of human organisation, and consequently almost infinitely variable. On the other hand, (and probably because there is no essential mechanical technology) educational institutions are characterised by strongly distinctive cultures and so amalgamations are exclusively amalgamations of culture and not of technologies. Problems of amalgamating educational institutions, therefore, are entirely ones of people and *all* the issues involved are subjective issues. There are no issues in such cases that are not in largest measure opinions or interpretations.

Education is a process; a process of human interaction. Process and the content of that process are subjective, selective and matters of opinion and preference. There is (almost) nothing in education that has any objectivity and there are no aspects of the educational process that can be said to be essential. On the other hand, in education there is a great deal of precedent, custom, practice and – opinion. No one who urges change in education can express other than a matter of personal opinion and hope. Hence, no organisational solution to an educational situation can be said to be 'right' per se. We can only express choices and preferences and if we have sufficient power we can impose these preferences on others.

It is important to understand the arbitrariness of decision making and solutions because there are no certain answers in education management except for a reasonable certainty that whatever we decide will turn out to be a mistake. However, if we can look for principles that help us to understand the processes that go on in human organisations we may be able to make better judgements and choices because they will be less opinionated. Furthermore, no arguments about the nature of meaning of education have any relevance whatever for the organisation of education. Opinions are merely part of the superstructure of the educational process. This will become clear when we discuss ideology later in the paper.

All amalgamations have causes and sometimes reasons. The causes are always outside the organisation itself and most often unsought. Few amalgamations occur between partners of perceived equality. Forming associations is not the same as an amalgamation. Associations are generally entered voluntarily and from a position of some individual strength for each partner. Associations provide a good model for amalgamations but do not have a formalised power structure. Amalgamations do not necessarily follow the model of association for federalism because one of the partners in an amalgamation almost always wishes to have overall power. Sometimes this power is delegated but there is an essential power difference between amalgamations and associations; this power difference is concerned with the bargaining process.

It is well understood that amalgamations involve power and coercion by the larger organisation over the smaller, but it is not always recognised that power confers no rights in itself. Once the merger has been agreed the responsibility of the larger on more powerful organisation is to recognise that a *new* organisation now exists (or, more correctly, a new organisational complex) and all the questions of management and organisation must be asked for the first time. Since the new organisation is not the old organisation every aspect of the new organisation is now open to question however unpalatable that may be. It may well be in practice that in an amalgamation the formerly lesser or weaker organisation is now potentially the stronger part. There seems to be here a fundamental questioning period in amalgamations that is almost invariably ignored — because amalgamations almost always take place pragmatically and never on considered theory.

The first problem for organisations is the problem of structure. Every new group worries about structure before anything else can be achieved. Organisations are likewise faced with the problems of structure long before anything is achieved. Here is the basic fallacy of management theory — that structure comes first. Structure is nothing other than a description of behaviour. If one describes how people behave in an organisation then one has described the 'structure'. There is no other meaning to the term structure in an organisational sense. Obviously structure is constantly changing hence all organisations have a perpetual problem over structure. Invariably structure is believed to be static and is fossilised in some sort of organisation chart. Unless nothing happens inside and outside the organisation there must be constant change in behaviour within the organisation and the structure must effectively change in smaller or greater degree. The pre-ocupation of those concerned with mergers is to get the structural matter decided early on — preferably before the amalgamation is in commission. Yet it is not possible to know how the structure will develop until well into the amalgamation. Generally, a number of unsatisfactory appointments are made whereby displaced people are given titles which allow them to think of themselves as being promoted while in practice they have been edged to the sidelines. Salaries is one of the matters at issue though it is by no means as significant as is generally believed. It should be perfectly feasible to design an interim period of organisational re-examination before the structural problems become as intractible as seems to be the usual case.

The real primary concern is not with structure but with cultures. As we explained, earlier amalgamations involve the bringing together of cultures. Cultures do not disappear on contact but rather enter into a survival phase. That is to say, the people who create the culture, freeze the characteristics and project their anxieties about their position in the new organisation into the process of maintaining the old culture. In many amalgamations we can see how cultural enclaves persist and members resist assimilation. Cultures (or sub-cultures as they have become in an amalgamated situation) are not of themselves dysfunctional. More often they are potentially highly functional because they provide an area of identity and since they have characteristics which derive from the members they include strengths as well as weakness.

Cultures are generally associated with locations. There are other cultures present in an organisation associated with other groups or sets

100

of members and some of these will be discussed later, but the initial problem of most amalgamations is with cultures based on location. For example, in one amalgamation it had been a custom never to start meetings before 9.30 a.m. in one former institution. Even after amalgamation, these members continued never to arrive until 9.30. They used their previously legitimated behaviour as a protest against the new institution. Because they were in line with previous behaviour, the protest was perceived to be in line with their custom – a custom from a culture now devalued and scorned. Yet it is a common error to assume that organisations have a common culture. All organisations are complexes of cultures many of them incompatable. Indeed, it is a weakness to attempt a common culture because the individual concessions required are demotivating and alienating. The strength of an organisation lies in the ways in which sub-cultures are blended and brought into harmony.

The cultural error arises from another common misconception about organisations, the idea that organisations can have common goals and values. To understand this point we must be clear about what an organisation is. An organisation may be called a firm, company, enterprise, institution or whatever but the essential characteristic of an organisation is that it is a collection of people who interact in a meaningful way over a period of time. "Organisation" is the "pattern-ing" of their behaviour and may be predictive or not. On the whole, we assume that organisation theory allows us to 'predict' as well as explain behaviour but organisation theorists must be open to the view that some (and possibly all) human behaviour in organisations may be unpredictable. This means that the idea that organisations have goals is untenable. In fact 'organisations' cannot have goals because goals are attributes of people and whatever people may do together "organi-sationally" (i.e. collectively) their aim is to achieve personal ends. And these personal ends (while not being organisational ends) have personal priority over anything that can be achieved "orgatisationally".

What happens in organisations is that powerful individuals transmute their personal goals into organisational goals and declare that every other member is bound by them. In this way, organisations are subject to ideology and rationalisation particularly on the part of bosses or, in the case of educational institutions, the ideology of the principal. As we said earlier, not only is there no one 'correct' structure for an institute of education but, since the nature of 'education' is a matter of opinion, the 'natural' state for an educational institution must be one of dynamic anarchy. Emergence from that state would be a power struggle and the operational consequences would be justified by individuals in subjective or ideological terms. It seems important, then, to understand that any 'structure' imposed on education is a deviation from a natural situation (perhaps this is the "essential technology" of education). Change to be effective must be in the direction of anarchy and not away from it. Since educational institutions tend towards over-administration, they are a long way from being effective.

Of course, there are strong reasons why educational institutions cannot be complete anarchies due to the circumstances in which they are funded and society is organised. But it must be understood that most management practice in education takes us away from understanding education as well as the nature of organisation. By anarchy I mean a state in which natural groupings are in conflict with imposed structure because no imposed structure can cope with the natural dynamics of interpersonal relationships.

If two chemical engineers disagree about a solution to a problem in a chemical process plant, there is only one choice that can be made. However, two teachers may disagree violently over the teaching of their subject but nothing need prevent both teaching in the same institution. The range of differences encompassed in educational institutions in practice as well as theory is immense. Indeed, differences within an institution are a potential source of creativity. Yet the most usual function of management is to reduce differences and to increase control over what goes on in the direction of uniformity and conformity. Dynamic, socially visible and career conscious (etc) principals move their organisations towards a common ideology, conformity and achievement in selected approved areas. They are impatient of differences and conflict (though they may claim otherwise) and punitive towards non-conformists. They aim to run institutions which have high public esteem and national reputation. On the other hand, they attract new staff because of the reputation of the institution and thus obtain more than their fair share of resources. In other words, principals who are themselves controversial tend to be impatient of controversy in their own organisations when it begins to challenge their own position. In this way the very people who were attracted to the organisation because they saw it as an exciting place are alienated when they discover that they are required to be supportive of the ideology and not critical within it.

The other extreme is the principal who has a weak educational ideology and compensates by a concern with administration. He reduces the institution to a process of procedural routines the performance of which is more highly valued than any other activity. He, too, rewards conformity and punishes non-conformity but for different reasons. While the one principal has misunderstood the nature of goals and needs, the other has misunderstood the nature of organisational structure and process. Since principals have virtually total power in their institutions we have to look for processes that will mitigate the baneful effect. The answer is only partly structural – and that is to take away formal structure. The nearer we can get to organisational anarchy the better and that means working in small groups of equal status in a very low pyramid of control. If positions are open to change with some regularity there is a chance that leaders will be more subject to organisational (i.e. collective) needs than personal ones. Thus principals may themselves be elected for periods of, say, five years. If principals were paid the same as section chairmen, they would come to understand what are the real administrative needs of the institution.

Leadership is only one function in organisation but where there is uncertainty about the tasks of the organisation leadership occurs by default and there is often a false leadership. "False leadership" is leadership that does not fulfil the real task needs of the organisation but displaces the real task by default because an initial vacuum has to be filled. The phenomenon is common in small groups and the question arises as to how common 'false leadership' is in larger organisations. In a state of uncertainty, anyone with firm and definite ideas is perceived as a saviour. However, since he brings his ideas and values with him to the organisation and does not derive them from it, his initial 'success' may well founder as the organisation finds its real needs and tasks. It is generally recognised that organisations require different forms of leadership in different phases of development (and these phases are sometimes very short, maybe even a few months) but it is less well understood how formal leadership may be dysfunctional or counter-productive. We are not speaking here of the obvious disasters and bad appointments but of the apparently successful appointments which somehow go wrong, where there is approval of the principal by the Governors and alienation on the part of the members of the institution. The more isolated and individualistic the principal, the greater the likelihood he will provide false leadership because he follows his own needs without regard for those of others.

As we said earlier, organisations are best thought of not as having goals or objectives but as serving purposes for their members. None of the individual needs of members may relate to one another but so long as they are congruent in terms of the tasks of the organisation, the organisation will be largely trouble free. Congruency of needs may lead to sharing of personal values and this is a condition of stability because it provides a supportive environment for the resolution of differences. When differences cannot be resolved there ensures a breakdown in functioning and extraneous problems and issues are imported to avoid facing conflict. As with false leadership so there is false activity. Most organisations spend a great deal of time on displacement problems — that is problems they do not really have but prefer to deal with at the expence of real problems. For example, a college takes a student count and worries about student absences, instead of discovering from the students who are present what *they* feel they are getting out of being *present*.

It seems very unlikely that many members of an organisation identify wholly with the organisation. Most are aware of what the organisation offers them and there are varying degrees of "loyalty". But one cannot be loyal to an organisation as an inanimate place, only to the people one relates to and only then in relation to others outside the organisation. Senior members of organisations often misunderstand their own reaction to the organisation, imagine that they have a greater stake or involvement than subordinates. In practice, they extend their fantasies as a justification for their greater control over other people. No member can have other than self interest in an organisation and no individual's contribution is 'organisationally' more important or even more significant than anyone else's. Either the organisation provides us with space for our needs, in which case we can do what we want without impediment, or it does not provide the space, in which case we are in conflict with someone else. If we use our 'position' to coerce the other person, we destroy some of the creativeness of the organisation in order to indulge oneself. A principal who believes he is organisationally more significant than another member misunderstands the nature of organisations — everyone is an equal part because that is the nature of organisations; there are no holes in organisations.

New principals are often brought into organisations as change agents. Traditionally a new boss creates a new organisation. How a new man behaves depends on his personality and management style but too often an appointing body is looking for a man with whose views they agree rather than a man with the requisite management skills. The point here is that there is no way in which a new man committed to an ideological interpretation of what an institution is for but also how it should be administered, controlled and directed can fill the expectations of *both* those who appointed him and his colleagues in the institution. The issue is the question of identifying the management characteristics that the situation demands. There are three classes of questioning concerned with:—

(1) the stages of development of the organisation
(2) the skills already available in the institution
(3) the personality of the appointee.

Organisations undoubtedly develop in certain ways though it is by no means clear what these phases are. Probably they pass firstly through a phase of newness and uncertainty when members are searching for roles and identity. This is followed by a phase of innovation and confidence with frenetic activity leading to a kind of fatigue and satiety. Then comes a period of consolidation followed by phases of disheartenment and then renewal. Certainly one can identify these phases after the event but possibly not always at the time. Another theory of development is via dependency, counterdependency, consolidation and innovativeness. An effective principal will encourage dependency and personal loyalty which the organisation can only become free of during a period of rebellion. After an assertion of independence, members are able to work together and eventually, in the fourth phase develop enough confidence to become innovative indivdually and in groups; the truly innovative organisation. Whatever development theory one espouses, it seems clear that bosses have to be responsive to the organisation rather than forcing the organisation to follow 'leadership'. This view is less quietist than may appear for a number of reasons.

As we have said, the principal is only one of many members. He brings the same kind of qualities to the organisation as the others and they have to be accommodated within the organisation. His needs can only be dealt with in concord with the needs of others and if he makes unreasonable demands others will suffer and the organisation will be upset. If he responds to the moods and needs of others he will obtain optimum personal return and also enhance the chances of others. Since whatever happens in an organisation is dependent on the nature of the organisation, innovation can only occur when members are sensitive to what is endemic to the organisation. Innovation is not achieved by importing ideas from outside but rather by understanding growth points in the organisation. Growth points are individual and collective needs — change is conditional upon opportunity.

For these reasons (and others) one may propose a generally desirable approach to management or management style. Since organisations are locations for processes to take place, and management is itself a process, the most appropriate management style is one that is itself a means of observing and monitoring processes. Such a method is 'counselling'. This must be the essential management function and all others derive from it. Counselling means listening to the other members and helping them to deal with their position in the organisation in the terms that are best for them. Managers behaving as Counsellors may not appear to be aggressively active but it is clear that such an approach is the only one consistent with fully understanding behaviour in organisations. It is the only way to help members to clarify their needs of the organisation and the only way they can be encouraged to make the kinds of demands that are necessary if they are to help the organisation to move actively in a mutually satisfactory direction.

Educational institutions have two main sectors of activity; the teaching function and the administrative function. The tendency is for administration to supplant teaching and for administrative problems to become displacement issues instead of the central problem of teaching. (It may, of course, be argued that educational institutions do not exist primarily for teaching but to provide emloyment. That argument is not contradicted here but it is not developed). Administration provides career as well as teaching opportunities and in Higher Education there is often a choice between which career ladder to follow. (Hence the argument on salary for Chief Administrative Officers). For most people, administrative activities are a substitute for teaching — perhaps a more satisfying one, but a replacement nevertheless since heads of department teach less than lecturers. Principals also concern themselves more with administration than teaching and doubtless they are right to do so. But the questions about administration and teaching are important at some level in the organisation and it is important to realise that the professional administrators have a quite different view of their job than the teachers. Almost certainly educational institutions are over-administered and the reason has much to do with status and career of administrators as well as local authority control (a form of bureaucracy). A direct effect of all this is to increase conformity, and encourage normative behaviour and consequently to discourage innovation and originality. As an organisation becomes more bureauratic it replaces a concern with tasks with a concern for procedures. These procedures are required overall and all sections of the organisation are required to conform whatever their relevance. Furthermore, administrators always believe they have good administrative reasons for their demands.

If the essential function of an educational institution be teaching there follow certain charactertistics of the members that are unlike those in many other organisations. Each teacher himself performs the total teaching function and an educational institution contains the same functions whether there be one teacher or a hundred. Even when teachers form teams the organisational requirements are little more. The concept may be expressed in terms of professionalism; each teacher is a professional and there are not required any hierarchic levels in the organisation for the functions to be performed. Furthermore, there is no basic and fundamental division of labour among teachers. Administrative needs are largely coordinative and regulative in a facilitative sense not restictive. Procurement of resources is an additional but not essential activity except for the recruitment of students. Few educational institutions fully recognise the implications of individual professionalism and are instead characterised by a power structure and a variety of forms of élitism. These superordinate accretions are open to re-evaluation but this never happens because status and salary are threatened. Almost invariably organisation in education means coercion by superiors. Yet specialism and expertise exists in the teaching function not the management/administrative function. Bosses, who are less expert, almost always try to lay down the requirement for subordinates who are more expert. Of course it is commonly believed that only good *teachers* are promoted to administration and only poor teachers remain unpromoted.

This is a pessimistic view but appears to be true in general though not everywhere. If we examine amalgamations we are aware of the urge to form a new institution that is welded together with common goals and values and so on, and these goals, values, etc., always derive from the principal and are always beyond real question. Of course that is the 'reality' of organisations. Those who can ally with the principal will be rewarded, others will be excluded or punished, at least negatively. While many members of the institution will accept such a situation as conforming to their experience of other organisations, the more creative members will require a more collegial form of decision-making. Principals who are not authoritarian by nature will be more able to help in developing such structures. Principalship is not "leadership" so much as reconsiliation, facilitating and guiding.

The problems of newly amalgamated organisations may be summarised as follows:—

1. Leadership problems. The extent to which the principal works to implement his own ideas or seeks to encourage other members to develop their own.
2. Structural problems. Developing structural solutions before problems have been defined. The tendency for positions to be established with high salaries attached which cannot be changed when they are no longer necessary. There is no such thing as a right or a permanent structure.
3. Misunderstandings of purposes. The assumptions that goals and objectives can be (and should be) agreed and adhered to by all 'loyal' members is mistaken. Organisations thrive on disagreement not accord.
4. Administrative problems. Allowing an administrative process to grow at the expense of the teaching function. Administrators have one vested interest – to increase administration.
5. Physical problems. Not recognising the importance of physical, and ideological differences. To allow them to grow is to use their potential strength. To pretend they can be ignored is to ignore

personal needs. Buildings can be more depressing than people, to some people.

6. Psychological problems. Each individual makes a range of psychological and irrational responses to the organisation. What may seem trivial to a principal may be vital to an individual. Recognise that human beings are essentially irrational and there are no rational solutions to organisational problems.

7. There are no objective reasons for doing anything in an organisation. Other solutions are always possible and almost always it will turn out that the decisions made were not the best. But it is better to know you are wrong than to believe you are right.

9.
An Organisational Design for a Technical College

I

This paper is presented for discussion concerning the organisational structure of the Gladwick Technical College*. It presents a single theoretical organisational model and examines some of the implications for practical application to GTC.

Organisation structure is essentially a management structure in that the function of management is to enable the tasks of the organisation to be performed optimally. All organisation designs express values—about organisations, about the behaviour of people in organisations and about the nature of management. Since there can be no single form of organisation each theoretical design is based on a value-laden model imbued with the perspectives and biases of the designer. There is a tendency for models of organisation theory to polarise towards the mechanistic and quantitative, or organic and qualitative. While all models have both quantitative and qualitative levels, in practice it is critical as to which bias is taken as the base. The model described here takes a psycho-sociological base as one which opens up more possibilities for organic change.

An organisation model is simply a way of describing how people relate and events occur in an organisational setting. It is predictive only in the sense that future events can be described in terms of the model. No model can be so complete that all events are described, but clearly the more events to be explained in terms of the model, the more satisfactory the model will be. The test of validity lies in the way the model deals with what is found to happen, not in terms of its internal logical consistency; in other words, it must deal with what actually happens not what is desired to happen.

A basic model is a series of parameters described in inter-relationship. A parameter is an arbitrarily selected aspect of organisational behaviour (i.e. open to definition) bearing some structural relation to other parameters. There are independent and dependent parameters according to their primacy in the logical developmental of the model. In all models the nature of dependency is open to argument. A model is a description of structure and structure is merely a description of behaviour; structure cannot exist independently of behaviour.

The independent parameters used in this model are task and careers.

The dependent parameters are membership, boundaries, purposes, roles, contract.

* A pseudonym
  The paper was written with the help of Janis Winkworth, Faculty Administrative Office, Anglian Regional Management Centre, Essex.

111

All organisations have a *Primary Task* or *Mission* (a cluster of related primary tasks) which they must fulfil in order to survive. Survival (in the sense of continued existence) is essential to all organisations though the tendency is for them to veer away from the primary task when under pressure. Furthermore, the primary task is not always clear because it changes over time due to market or environmental changes while the concerns of the members may remain the same. While the task itself may be dealt with in terms of short term objectives, the organisation itself has no "objective" other than to continue in existence. Because the continued existence of the organisation is necessary for the members it is useful to describe the organisation as "serving purposes"—that is, the interests of the members. The fulfilment of primary task and purposes served may be incompatible.

Organisations may be described in terms of *careers*. Organisations themselves change over time and eventually cease to be, but they also exist to provide career opportunities for members. An organisational career is possible by means of the job opportunities provided by a single organisation; a personal career is the working life of an individual which may take place in several organisations sequentially. Career *opportunities* are a structural aspect of organisations, and relate primarily to the task of the organisation and only secondarily to the person. Membership of the organisation relates to career opportunities as well as to task activities.

Boundaries are the physical and psychological limits which surround the activities of the Primary Task. Boundaries are determined by Membership. *Membership* is all those people necessary for the accomplishment of the Primary Task and Purposes. Some members are temporary (such as customers and clients), some full-time such as employees. Boundaries are always uncertain and permeable because membership can never be completely determined.

Roles are descriptions of the relationships between and among individual members of the organisation. Roles are highly complex and are based on relationship to the primary task and the career needs of the individual as well as personal dispositions. Roles are not definitive and have a different meaning for everyone in the organisation even when they sometimes would 'appear' to be 'the same'.

Contract — or more properly 'psychological contract' — is the relationship individuals have with others in the organisation and determines their commitment to the Task. Because contract is made at the psychological level and is continuously (sic) renegotiated unilaterally it presents the parameter of greatest uncertainty in organisational functioning and is the area causing the greatest

112

problems. In structural terms it is impossible to pinpoint but is a major dynamic in the process of organisational change.

For the Primary Task to be performed a number of *facilitating activities* must take place. These are the procurement of resources, recruitment of members, disposal of surpluses, maintenance of the task system, monitoring the change process as the organisation responds to outside pressures. The performance of these facilitating activities raises questions of power, authority and leadership. It is important to understand that these subsidiary tasks and issues are organisational and not individual or role matters. In broad terms, the facilitating activities may be termed the management or administrative tasks — functions of the organisation not specific tasks for individuals.

The starting point for organisational design is the nature of the Primary Task. The technology of Primary Task performance is the skeletal frame of the design. However, not all Primary Tasks are mechanical processes; in some instances a mechanical process is only a part of the organisational task, in others there is no mechanical process at all. In the latter case, confusion often arises because the facilitative process (which is tangible) is substituted for the task process (which is intangible). Banking and Insurance are examples of situations where the salience of the facilitative process as experienced in the office, tends to replace the Primary Task of providing insurance cover which is dependent on securing customers. Hospitals are a clear example of technology/administration almost totally superceding the Primary Task or Health Care. Where there is no obvious technology, there is a strong likelihood of one being invented.

Where there is no mechanical Primary Task, the starting point for design is the nature of membership — the client/customer relationship to employees of the organisation. To take again the Health Service as an example, the relationship between nurses/doctors and patients in the Primary Task of Health Care suggests ways in which this task may be facilitated without importing traditional assumptions about how hospitals are organised. The task of Health Care is quite different from the task of dealing with institutionalised sickness.

In applying behavioural science principles to this organisation model, the assumption is made that staff and certainly teaching staff, really do wish a high degree of autonomy and freedom. This may not in practice be so; indeed there is evidence that many teachers prefer to be in highly controlled and regulated situations — the conventional view of F.E. teachers? The view proposed here would require a major value shift in both the nature of teaching and courses offered, and the kind of person recruited to teach. The emphasis now would be on individuals desiring autonomy and freedom and with a high need for personal achievement.

113

II

We can now apply the theory to an educational institution, specifically the Gladwick Technical College. It is taken as axiomatic that GTC is an educational institution though such an assumption must be open to discussion. Should another definition be axiomatic, the model would remain the same but the developed design would be different. We may, however, assume that terms like 'education' and 'training' carry a similar meaning.

The Primary Task of an educational institution is teaching – or, more correctly, the provision of teaching-learning situations, or even just learning situations. The basic situation for teaching is a personal relationship between teachers and students and for this there is no essential mechanical technology. Hence organisational design cannot start from a technological analysis but from an examination of membership.

The core membership of an educational institution is teachers and students. The relationship between these two membership groups requires a location but no other territorial specifics. In practice, however, physical provision is made in terms of buildings and the availability of these buildings is the main determinant on size of membership. A secondary determinant may, or may not be, financial provision. If then the task of an educational institution is teaching and the membership concerned with this Primary Task is determined by accommodation available then the task of management/administration is to facilitate this primary task, and the other purposes served by management are subsidiary and subservient.

Within the membership – teachers, students, administrators, ancillary supporters etc. – there is a hierarchy of importance that relates to the nature of the task. This importance derives from the nearness of membership to the performance of the Primary Task. Clearly the teachers are at the top of the hierarchy because they create the teaching/learning situation and the recruitment of the second rank of members, students, depends on what the teachers offer. An educational institution would exist if one teacher offered his services to students in one room.

Because the teaching/learning situation depends basically on the teacher – his skill, competence, knowledge – the teacher is the key 'professional' in the institution. This suggests that organisational design should centre on the teaching role as the prime function. Additionally, this function depends on personal factors in that while there is a primary teaching function the expression of this function is individualised in specialisms offered by each teacher, as well as personal teaching style.

114

In a highly technological system, skill behaviour of individual members is depersonalised by the mechanical process but in teaching (perhaps even more than in the other 'professions' of medicine and the law, but not the church), the task contribution which the teacher makes is highly personal and subjective — in the discipline areas and emphasis he offers, in teaching 'style' and personality.

When the key professionals are gathered together in an institution, the need arises for creation, definition and maintenance of boundaries in terms of membership. That is, in order for the Primary Task of teaching to be performed, clients have to be recruited into the organisation in relation to what the teachers are competent to offer. Additionally, they need to be in continual contact with other professionals for updating their knowledge and expertise. Recruitment and updating are two of the boundary spanning functions that must be performed if the Primary Task of teaching is to progress. Some of this boundary spanning is institutional (i.e. on behalf of the institution) and some personal (that is, on behalf of the individual teacher). The administrative function of the institution will be to facilitate these boundary spanning activities either by providing personnel with that responsibility or enabling teachers to engage in the boundary spanning. Whether teachers do this or not will be based on criteria concerned with teaching needs rather than administistative convenience.

In this interpretation of the model, the individual teacher is the key factor and the question arises as to whether teachers can be left to function as individuals or need to be organised differently. There seems to be no inherent reason why teachers should not be allowed to function individually for in practice teachers do function with a great deal of autonomy. However, they also tend to band together in groups, often *ad hoc,* on the basis of similar subject interests, similar personal interests, similar educational values, similar sector interests and so on. Organisational design must accept that while bonding occurs it is not universal or uniform or perpetual and hence a preferred structure is likely to be inconsistent and irrational. Organisational design must allow the bonding to occur in groupings that arise from teacher concerns and activities not from equally irrational imposition from above or outside.

Another factor in membership and group forming is the career opportunities provided by the organisation. New teachers will be recruited because they see opportunities to do what they want to do — in terms of subjects, level of work, type of student, sector of interest. Whatever group structures exist, they will provide the opportunities for new members. It is likely that groups will consist of from 5 to 8 individuals and these groups will function optimally if there are no

115

questions of formal status to contend with because each individual, even in close interest groups, is his own expert and authority. Theories of group behaviour suggest that groups of this size can manage themselves very well if allowed to function informally in otherwise formal organisations.

Because each of these groups forms a primary organisational unit, as much resource and ancillary assistance should be allocated to individual groups as is reasonable. Thus financial support will be allocated on a simple per capita formula and secretarial 'assistance' will be allocated as an aspect of full team membership. Status positions will be significant only insofar as salary is concerned and is understood in terms of individual careers and recruitment rather than an aspect of group functioning. Thus a Principal Lecturer is such by virtue of his career development not by virtue of his membership of a task work group.

Certain other functions will by virtue of their complexity or universality be central support functions. There will be a central gatekeeping function – the personification to the public at large of the institution. It includes Reception, Head of the Institution, physical maintenance of the property, overall budgetary control, relationships with other insitutions, some aspects of recruitment and procurement, general client services. Many of these central functions, however, will be exercised by groups and group members themselves – for example, much correspondence and publicity.

Additional needs within the organisation are concerned with the problems arising from the renegotiation of the psychological contract (matters of morale, commitment, motivation and personal needs) and the linking of interests and concerns between and among groups, a coordinating function. There is a danger that the coordinating function becomes separated from the needs of the Primary Task as a displacement activity by disaffected individuals and also that it becomes a power vacuum enabling individuals near to or distant from the Primary Task to exercise coercion over others. It is desirable that power should derive from the needs of the Primary Task* not from a manipulation of the rewards and punishment latent in the managerial and administrative functions.

Visually, the model can be described in the following diagrammatic form:–

---

* In the Tavistock model (A. K. Rice: Bruce Reed) the term "authority" is used to refer to power that derives from Prime Task functioning. Neither power or authority properly exist or are exercised apart from Basic Task functioning.

116

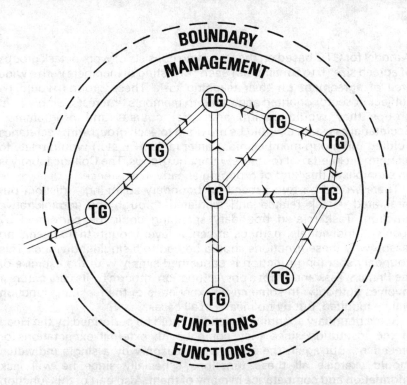

TG= Task Group plus Task Administration

TG = Task Group
    + task administration.

In applying the principles of the model to an actual organisation, it is essential to recognise the realities of organisational functioning. We all have fantasies about what happens in our organisations which are full of logical inconsistencies. Thus a senior member of staff may imagine that he makes all the decisions for his section when the reality is quite different. The reality of organisations lies in what is observed to happen and the recognition of discrepancies in interpretation or explanation between members. Paradoxically, one aspect of reality is individual members' fantasies. In reading what follows, and applying to a specific organisation, an attempt to examine possible other realities is required—it may be that the 'model' is more accurate in its designation of behaviour than the reader's own recollections and interpretations.

117

III

A model for GTC based on the foregoing consists of work or task groups of agreed size (5 to 8 members) each consisting of members with a wide area of agreement on their teaching task. These groups would be subject or sector oriented according to members' interests. Singly or in groups they would design and offer courses and programmes. Secretarial assistance would be provided to each group with secretaries holding full group membership. Career ranks (PL etc.) would relate to recruitment needs not to status within the groups. The College Library is an example of this kind of grouping already in existence.

There would be two aspects of boundary spanning — distinct but integrated — task related and mediated through the administrative function. Task related boundary spanning could be performed by specified individuals, perhaps at senior level though there seems no reason why these functions should be tied to a single individual. This boundary spanning function is concerned simply with the exercise of the Primary Task and is not a power function, though by its very nature it involves authority. In some cases experience of the teaching function will be required, but by no means in all cases.

Some boundary spanning functions could be performed by the Head of the Institution since they comply with external expectations or precedent. But again there seems no reason why a single individual should exercise all these functions especially since he will lack information and competence in many of them. Also part of this function are the Registrar's functions and the Chief Administrative Officer's. In terms of the model the roles of Principal and Chief Administrative Officer are not distinct. All roles can be shared and there is no reason why job activities could not be negotiated. Responsibility can be defined in terms of job definition — apportionment of jobs should include responsibility. It is both illogical and impractical to delegate (share) a job and not to delegate full responsibility. The problem of defining jobs/activities in an already existing organisation is that people are already working in a power structure and any reorganisation is bound to change that structure. Furthermore, external expectations may be seen as restraints militating against change. The question here is whether present incumbents see (and wish to maintain) themselves in a power relationship with others. It is certainly dysfunctional for power to be referred to individuals peripheral to the Prime Task — one of the current malfunctionings in the present role of Principal.

The management or administrative function is concerned with supporting the Primary Task, or teaching. This is its anchor purpose though it additionally serves a number of personal purposes such as employment, satisfaction, control and so on in practice. For many individuals engaged in the administrative function, their job will become to them the 'primary task' — that is, they will see the maintenance and performance of their task, in their way, as that which they wish to protect and preserve. Hence the desirability of moving administrative jobs as near to the Primary Task as possible — that is, into the working groups. Thus secretaries will belong to groups though the arrangement for hiring and engaging them may be centralised (along with any necessary dismissals).

Central administrative tasks would appear to be admissions of students (as a process) including technical problems of admission and qualifications, grants etc.; overall budgetary control; ordering and invoicing; petty cash and travelling expenses; central (LEA) finances, and registry matters; servicing Academic Board and some working parties; technician services; co-ordination of publicity; resources and room allocation; caretaking. Additionally, residential services would be administered centrally.

Thus co-ordinating meetings would be required; an Academic Board and a Staff Meeting. Academic Board would be open to all academic (i.e. teaching staff) and would deal with all matters concerning teaching. The staff meeting would be open to all staff and would be concerned with non-academic matters. Secretaries and technicians may or may not be *ad hoc* members of Academic Board. Both these meetings would set up working parties without prejudice to group meetings. Executive function is defined as the implementation of decisions by an individual on behalf of himself or an individual as agreed representative of others. There is no executive function by any other right except where legal requirements are imposed from outside (e.g. trust requirements or membership of other bodies). There is no unilateral executive authority for anyone where his actions concern or involve others.

The model here outlined is a collegial model of an educational institution which holds at its core the concept that teaching is an individual activity often performed in collective situations. Normal models for Further and Higher Education (apart from universities) are power/authority and bureaucratic models. There is no suggestion that these other models always fulfil their potential for dysfunctionalism but both of them place control and administrative convenience as the primary task and hence are unsuitable for educational institutions. In practice, one finds educational institutions either moving towards increased bureaucratisation or towards a more organic structure. At present GTC is nearer the organic than the bureaucratic and the present proposals are concerned to move it in one direction instead of the other.

It is, of course, true that external expectations of an educational institution are based on Traditional and Mechanistic models. Such models are hierarchic and power distribution is from the top down. Such models have a persistent (but misconceived) appeal because those in senior positions are motivated to hold such positions as means of fulfilling their own power needs, often expressed as at last having an opportunity to do things as they ought to be done. It should be remembered that the need to control and direct events sometimes originates in lack of freedom in previous institutions. The model here suggested is a means of redressing the situation. Should, however, it be hypothesised that teachers do not want or are incapable of using freedom then a model based on different values from the present will have to be developed.

In the case of GTC, there is the additional factor of the split site. The principle here would be to develop each site as a separate institution in the first instance and then to discuss what kinds of linking mechanisms were required in practice. To assume that a communication structure can be devised before the membership inter-relates is to start on an improper basis because only in practice can it be discovered how people in actuality behave. For example, domestic location has already a significant effect on all staff behaviour in relation to the two sites — the reality is not adequately described in the present 'structure'. Administrative support, on a split site, has a large mechanistic aspect and presents different problems but easier solutions (e.g. mail/communication delivery) than the human aspects.

10.
Staff Development

Staff Development lies in the area of concern where the needs and interests of the individual come into relationship with the needs and opportunities of the organisation of which he is a member. Any interpretation that we make of Staff Development will derive from a view or theory of organisations and our particular understanding of educational and personal psychology. At one extreme are those who see the needs of the organisation as paramount and over-riding and, at the other, those who see organisations as having no other purpose than to satisfy the personal needs of individuals. It may be argued that neither extreme is, in practice, so far from the other as at first seems since no organisation can function without the commitment of its members while no individual can be an effective member of an organisation without making a commitment to other members and such a commitment can only be expressed in organisational terms.

It is useful to distinguish three levels of organisational activity. The first level is the level of the technology of the organisation. Some organisations have a complex and over-riding technical system such as chemical process plants where the structure of the organisation is basically dependent on the physical technology of chemical manufacture. Within a given technical structure there are a limited number of basic variations, of course, though the organisation must be able to accommodate new developments in the manufacturing process itself.

The second level is that of administration which is the routine activities by which people work the basic technology. This can be described in the usual jargon of firms and companies where the technical tasks are expressed in terms of the jobs people have to do in order for the primary technical tasks to be performed. The tendency for organisations is to reduce the number of people involved in the primary technical tasks and to increase the number of people in secondary administrative tasks. Technical developments tend to decrease the number of people employed at the primary task but to increase the number of people employed in administrative and support activities.

The third level of organisational activity is concerned with the social and interpersonal relationships which go to make up the culture of the organisation and from which the particular 'ethos' of the organisation derives. This is the level at which people 'experience' membership, for when we think of an organisation we almost invariably think of the people there, the personal atmosphere of the place.

Organisations find problems arising at all three levels but they become increasingly difficult as they move up through the levels. Problems have to be solved at all three levels but are most intractible at the psycho-social level. The reason for this is that each member has a very personal view of the organisation—his perspective which is entirely

123

coloured by his previous experience, his understanding of his own needs and his personal value system. Disputes in organisations are always about perceptions or fantasies and never about shared realities. (Of course, for each individual, his perceptions are the reality). The only practical reality in organisations arises from some consensus or congruence among groups of individuals so that the greatest reality is congruence among the greatest number of people.

A fundamental problem in any discussion of Staff Development is that each member perceives the organisation in some way differently from anyone else and his view of what are Staff and Organisational needs is subjective. An important area of question is around who sees "more clearly" needs within the organisation for it does not follow that any one position in the organisation provides more clarity of vision and understanding than any other. For this reason there can be no overall supervision of staff development from a single position in the organisation. Nevertheless, Staff Development does not occur spontaneously — or rather, it does occur spontaneously but by default and not design — and yet, it is the most important single aspect of management in any organisation; the more complex the organisation, the more complicated the nature of Staff Development.

If we return to the three levels of organisational activity it is clear that one requirement of staff development is concerned with increasing people's competence in the performance of the primary tasks. In education, this is teaching (however this may be eventually defined). Alongside learning to be more competent must also come learning to be open to new competencies required when the basic technology develops as a result of practice, research and innovation. It seems, however, most likely that learning material competence is not the first requirement though this has been traditionally considered to be the case with industrial training. A prior condition to learning technical competence is the affective attitude towards the skills, the emotional orientation. A teacher's openness to change is a basic starting attitude to understanding his tasks; it does not develop as a natural consequence to changed circumstances. Training tends — certainly in manufacturing industries — to be concerned with teaching the "right" way to do a job. Organisational values that include "the right way" also include conformity, rigidity and dependency in their culture or ethos; these values are conservative and unreceptive to change influences.

Individual personality develops long before an individual joins an employing organisation and people try to choose occupations that are compatible with their personality needs. But an organisation that has conformist values and recruits members accordingly cannot expect such people to respond willingly and easily to organisational demands for creative change. Equally, organisations that recruit creative and imaginative people cannot expect them to be easily biddable and quiescent towards authority. All organisations have the dilemma that both conformist and unconformist members are required. At every level of management each individual has to discover the best mix of conformity and creativity. The nearer an individual comes to top management the more the organisation *needs* him to be creative and independent but the more it coerces him to be uncontroversial and conformist—though conformity within a top management team may be of a different kind from that required elsewhere in the same organisation. Each organisation has to work out in its own way how these conflicts are resolved but the more simple or monolithic the organisation (and the more authoritarian) the more difficult will it be for the two conflicting sets of needs to be accommodated.

No management activity in an organisation is neutral or value free and it is totally unrealistic to assume that a Staff Development programme is not a potent aspect of the power struggle that characterises all organisations. No theory of organisations and no pseudo theory of management discounts the importance of conflict in organisations. Conflict, it may be said, is the dynamic of organisation. If one describes an organisation in terms of where people are and what they are doing*, their activity which is, of course, a process of change, is the result of the latent and actual conflicts that they attempt to resolve and/or accommodate. Staff Development may thus be defined as a systematic effort by mangement to deal with organisational conflict in such a way as to give greater satisfaction to individuals and to smooth the administrative processes as a consequence.

We need to turn now to the second level of organisation which is administration (or bureaucracy). Administration is all the procedures that are routinised in order that the primary task(s) may be most satisfactorily fulfilled. Administrative activity is the most visable activity of any organisation because it is what the observer sees. It is manifest in all the things observed to be going on among the members—meetings, memos, reporting, gathering together and dispersing, sending instructions, hiring and firing and so on. Most books of mangement are about these kinds of activity. Behind them, the primary task of the organisation is often obscured even when there would appear to be a tangible product of the firm.

---

* This is the definition of "structure".

Membership of an organisation can be described in terms of an individual's career†. An organisational career is a map of progress through the organisation in terms of time, location, position, and status. Each individual joins an organisation for career purposes—to further his own career—and he will seek to ensure that his membership gives him the kinds of returns or rewards that he most values. In order to obtain a greater reward he may be prepared to endure some lesser privations but his essential concerns will be ones of self interest. We cannot assume that altruism is anything other than a form of self-interest. When organisational needs are seen to over-ride individual needs, acceptance becomes a consequence of coercion. It is important to understand that though one must talk of 'the organisation' as if it were an impersonal thing, in fact, the organisation is always an individual or coalition of individuals. A statement such as "The school cannot permit teachers to leave classes unattended" is a sentiment of a real individual not an impersonal entity. Even 'decisions' made by large bodies have to be understood as completely subjective and not neutral views deriving from an impartial entity. All decisions made about Staff Development are made subjectively and to further the interests of some group or individuals as part of the power structure of the organisation.

To accept the reality of organisational conflict and the problems of power and authority is to go a long way to mitigating their bad effects. The most pernicious stance of members of an organisation is to deny the existence of conflict and the provenance of power and authority. It is equally dysfunctional to refuse to resolve the issues by substituting other issues for the substantive ones though this is exactly what characteristically happens.

The organisational membership of each individual is a state which can work either to the good of the individual and the organisation or against the good of the individual and the organisation. Staff Development programmes aim to increase the satisfaction of individuals in the expectation that satisfied (happy?) individuals make far greater satisfaction (happiness?) for other individuals and hence, a better (happier?) organisation ensues. This means that as an ultimate consequence the aforementioned issues of conflict, power and authority are resolved for that individual. Although many of the activities of Staff Development do not centre on these issues, as an essential aspect of management they lead to resolving the basic problems of human organisation.

---

† See my paper, "LEAS need new ideas on recruitment and promotion" for a fuller explanation "Education Management" Supplement to 'Education' 29 March 1974.

The term 'management' has been used here in distinction to administration. I define administration as concerned with routinised tasks, the daily procedures of organisation; the purpose of administration is facilitative—it is to help in the performance of the primary task. Management, I define as the problem solving activity in an organisation. Hence, management is a function shared by members and is also an aspect of administration from time to time. However, management often means, in practice, the control function of an organisation where control does not mean, in practice, the function of moderation but rather the function of administration. Authoritarian management has a host of distinctive problems because it often derives from a particular personality or temperament. Management styles are, of course, a function of personality but an authoritarian form of management is not well suited to organisations where, in practice, the "authority" of expertise is a shared function. For example, authoritarian management is impossible in research departments, creative agencies and groups of 'professionals' because the authority of the primary task technology is a shared quality deriving from expertise. On the other hand, authoritarianism is highly suited to situations where members have little or no expertise. The problem of teaching is that at the beginning the situation is one where the teacher has expertise and the students do not, but as learning progresses students gain expertise and may well gain greater expertise than their teachers. Educational institutions have tended to get stuck at the stage of un-shared expertise when they 'ought' to be organised on the basis of shared expertise. An organisation is in great difficulty when the management values are at odds with the values of the technology. If schools, for example, are aiming for values that involve sharing, mutuality, caring, respect for individuals, academic values and an intellectual culture, to organise them in authoritarian ways is counterproductive and sets up unresolved conflict in the minds of students. There are other ways of being supportive of immaturity and learning than pure authoritarianism. Colleges of Adult Education are managed on a different set of values from the traditional technical college. One of the dilemmas for the polytechnics is that they have inherited many of the old Technical College values at a time when the basic tasks relate more closely to those of the (traditional) university. In fact, the polytechnics have not yet found an appropriate set of values for the kind of work they have been doing and now that even newer tasks are imminent, the need for an appropriate culture is urgent. Another way of expressing the issue is to say that it is concerned with coercion and freedom. If education be liberation, can it be brought about by coercion?

The primary task, then, of an educational institution is teaching.

127

However we define education, the way in which it takes place is by learning and teaching. We must consider the terms 'teaching' and 'learning' to be aspects of the same process. The administrative functions of an educational institution are to facilitate learning and teaching. People join an educational institution in order to help in the promotion of their primary activity. The kind of teaching that goes on determines the organisational culture. We can see this most clearly if we look at an Infant School or an Adult Education College. The values which underpin activity are quite clear in these kinds of educational institution (and often much less so in other kinds of school or college).

For our present purposes we can discount the development needs of students because we can assume that their needs are covered in the teaching structure. Students also have a different technical relationship or contract with the organisation from teachers. Also we must in practice make a distinction between those member functions which are on the one hand related to the teaching or academic function and, those related to the service functions. (We may define service functions as those activities which would have to go on in the buildings etc. whatever the primary task). There are, of course, overlaps and unclear distinctions but, at the present point in the discussion, I shall refer to teachers as those concerned with the educational purposes of the institution.

A teacher joins a school or college for a set of personal reasons and purposes. Most probably, he joins because he wants to be a teacher though he may well join because he wants to achieve something else and teaching is a means to this other end. We should not discount other motives. His hope will be that he will fit into the organisation and that he will be able to change the organisation in some way to suit himself; certainly he will hope to increase the influence he has over his own situation as the days and years go by. If he gets what he believes he wants he will stay on; if he does not get what he wants he will leave; if he cannot manage to leave or leaving has too many other problems associated with it, he will come to some accommodation with the organisation; such "accommodation" may include active disaffection*.

An organisation receiving a new individual becomes changed in some way. Members have to accommodate themselves to a newcomer who is always a threat to someone already there. The newcomer relates, of course, not to an impersonal organisation but only to people in it. If he is 'creative' he will make friends and enemies; if he is not creative he will

---

* For a fuller discussion of this idea see my 'On Starting a New Job'. Journal of Occupational Psychology 1975, No. 48 pp. 33–37.

128

make mostly friends. Critical for creative newcomers are the friends they make and the status in the organisation of those friends. Bad management encourages the divisions that now develop between people: good management attempts healing. The process of induction, accommodation and healing is the process of Staff Development.

We can think of Staff Development on a line from Personal Concerns to Organisational Concerns. At the one end (Personal Concerns) are the pastoral functions, the personal care of staff, and at the other are the organisational concerns with innovation and change. Of course, everything is inter-related and 'retro dependent' in that as one aspect of need is dealt with so another comes back to the fore. So, we can say, Staff Development is concerned with all those needs of the individual that relate to his membership of the organisation, and all the needs of the organisation as they affect and make demands on individuals. We are talking, then, about the *essential* "administrative" function that facilitates the management function — though we need to think in terms of processes rather than discrete activities.

At one extreme, Staff Development is concerned with those matters of personal concern which might be termed personal 'pastoral' needs. In some companies this was developed as a Welfare Function but it is better thought of as more than that and as almost identical to the counselling provision made by Student Services in schools, colleges, universities and polytechnics. At the other extreme, is training in the administrative and management aspects of the institution: the activities that go with the jobs that have to be done by members in order to 'maintain the institution'. As a person moves to new positions in the organisation he needs to learn new procedures and techniques. Even from his first arrival, he needs to learn the particular ways in which things are done and this is part of the essential induction process.

Fundamental to all that goes on in Staff Development is a need to develop the individual in a personal way. This may be termed 'personal development' or 'personal growth' but it tends to be overlooked because it appears to be less tangible (and less capable of manipulation) than organisational matters. We need to recall that within organisations there will be general preference for conformism and effort will be directed towards helping people to fit into the culture. Personal Growth is concerned with the discovery of greater personal independence or autonomy and, therefore, tends to threaten other people. Here is another of the dilemmas of organisation. Organisations will only thrive if people are encouraged to self-fulfilment but people who try to fulfil themselves come at odds with the organisation. Hence a measure of organisational health is the extent to which it can accommodate variances, differences and deviation. A problem with systematic approaches to Staff Development is that almost by definition they find it difficult to accommodate deviance and the unanticipated.

It is for reasons such as this that the wider term Organisation Development has come into use in recent years. Organisation Development is concerned with helping the 'organisation' to change and adapt with implications for the organisational structure. In practice, Organisation Development works with individuals and uses the techniques of personal counselling and personal growth skills, group training and so on but the target is organisational change. For example, organisation development would be concerned with developing teams and discovering new ways of running departments and meetings. It would focus on changing individual and group behaviour and relationships, and move the culture of the organisation away from an authoritarian climate to a collaborative, collegial ambience. To some managers, organisational approaches are a personal threat and embody a counter ideology. A test of the validity of Organisation Development would be to match its values with those of the primary technology so that we would ask "Are the values we express in our teaching the same as those we express (or wish to express) in our management?" and vice versa. An organisation with an authoritarian ethos would, of course, use organisational development as a means of reinforcing the authoritarian mode of relating but, of course, could not in any way avoid issues of conflict. In my own view, Organisation Development (OD)* approaches are more realistic about the nature of conflict than authoritarian and traditional approaches to Staff Development. But authoritarian institutions tend to ignore the potential for conflict by wishing it away until there is a major catastrophe when blame can be reapportioned to historical accident.

Although all organisations have a distinctive culture and public image, there is rarely a case when all the members subscribe to that culture. Often familiarity with organisation simply shows up the great gulf between fantasy and reality. Benign institutions are seen to be oppressive and dictatorial organisations are experienced as benevolent. Large organisations can accommodate a vast range of personal differences and ideologies so long as there is no active friction at critical boundaries. Fundamentalist evangelicals can work very well with atheistic liberals until issues of religious coercion arise. Formal and

---

* The abbreviated form 'OD refers to a particular form of management style that focusses on the psychological problems of an organisation. There seems to be no way of avoiding confusion over the rather different meanings of the terms "Organisation Development" and "Organisational Development."

experiential methods can exist side by side until one attempts to progress from the one to other or to use them inter-changeably. The reconciliatory function of management must use techniques of personal counselling and OD to satisfactorily resolve such confrontations because they occur in terms of real people and not just abstract ideas. Too often in educational institutions plans for new courses go awry simply because juxtapositions that look acceptable on paper become incompatible once they are expressed in people's behaviour. Almost any scheme which appears logical on paper will be found to be flawed when it comes to practice. It seems as if there is a pattern of behaviour that is different from the pattern of mechanical reasoning.

It is too often forgotten that change is in the nature of organisations. Most management behaviour is based on a time-slice or snap-shot perception of the organisation and can never deal with the realities that have since transpired. At the very worst some management ideas assume that organisations do not change. But natural change cannot be entirely predicted and good management is concerned with the unpredictable. "Natural" change cannot be diverted against its inclination – not that one can ever know beforehand the inclination – and the nature of change may be unwelcome without respect to person or position. All organisations have a natural conservatism as well as a natural tendency to change. Conservative and change forces are spread throughout the organisation but the force to remain the same is always the strongest. It is easy to see why this should be so for otherwise an organisation would have no stability and energy would be dissipated in hundreds of fads and whims. Sound management uses the forces of conservatism as fully as the forces for reform – but it does use both. Staff Development must, therefore, have as much meaning for keen innovating members as for cautious stabilising members.

If organisations change, they also follow broad patterns of change. Reform and consolidation are recurrent phases occuring in a constant sequence and it is useful to know which of the phases an institution is in. But, there are also fits and starts which are less manageable; sudden rushes of enthusiasm that never become consolidated; false rushes into new territory which leave wounds that never quite heal; false enthusiasms on matters that are a substitute for and an avoidance of critical situations. There is sometimes talk of organisational renewal when the real issue should be to allow organisational death. Perhaps the most neglected aspect of organisational behaviour is the need to let die. We need more complete terminations and more total recommence-ments than most organisations are able to cope with. Organisations are littered with vestiges of former structures which serve no purpose other than to frustrate new and demanding activities. Only an organisational perspective on Staff Development can begin to cope with this area of management problem.

I am quite convinced that the key to adaptability, coping, innovating and so on, so far as the individual is concerned, is Personal Development by which I mean help with one's own maturity, the growth process as we pass through life. The persistent problems of managers always arise out of their own personal immaturity and it may even be the case that the need for status and social esteem leading to ambition for a high position is a consequence of personal immaturity (though it would be difficult to imagine a society in which no one accepted positions of leadership). This is not to say that lack of ambition is a sign of maturity — to have no drive and personal ambition is equally immature. But it may well be that institutions encourage the dependent rather than the autonomous individual and often headship does not give the esteem and companionship that is desired. In any case, anyone who reaches a position of power is in danger of abusing it unless he has strong, restraining support from a reference group.

We cannot, in considering Staff Development, ignore the special problems of those in command or in power positions within the organisation because they are caught in the midst of organisational demands with which they may or may not be in sympathy and which influence personal needs, inclinations and dispositions. Heads of sections, departments etc. are in especially vulnerable positions because they are at stress points in the organisation, at boundaries or interfaces between culturally competing groups. Organisational demands on individuals at these interfaces are always unjust because they treat the individual as an object — the personification of the collective link of his department or unit. Heads receive less help and are subject to more demands than other members and few have the skills to deal with the objectified conflict endemic to their position.

It must be clear from what I have said that Staff Development is not a function that can be hived off to a single department or unit. Staff Development is a conscious response to the working of the organisation and therefore is everyone's responsibility. But, of course, resources are not evenly and equally distributed throughout the organisation and inevitably some structural provision has to be made to ensure that a sensibly comprehensive provision for Staff Development occurs. How large such a unit is and what resources are allocated to it depends on the size of the organisation and the nature of the tasks that have to be undertaken. There is, too, a question about the relationship of Staff Development to the senior directorship and any 'official' organisation "policy". While it would be dysfunctional for the Staff Development Unit to be a crude instrument of higher management, it should be possible for it to function with close links with the 'directorate' but with considerable freedom within the cultural values of the organisation which derive, as I have already illustrated from education, from the ethos appropriate to the primary tasks.

The facilitation of Staff Development includes organisational and personal needs but works through individuals and groups of individuals. Structural changes will almost inevitably occur as a consequence but structural change cannot be imposed as if behaviour was a consequence of structure. "Structure" is the dynamic of relationships and, therefore, is a consequence of behaviour not the cause of it. To understand this is a primary condition for understanding organisations for it also is the basis for a critique of management theories. Because we cannot look for structural solutions to the problems of organisations, we need to clarify those matters of group and personal need that are the substance of Staff Development, remembering that almost all organisational (and management) activity is part of the process of staff development.

PERSONAL AND ORGANISATIONAL PHASES OF STAFF DEVELOPMENT

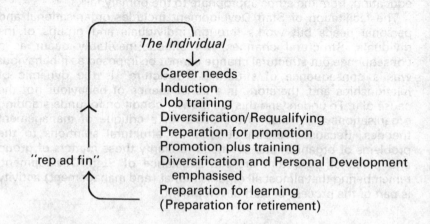

The Individual

↓

Career needs
Induction
Job training
Diversification/Requalifying
Preparation for promotion
Promotion plus training
Diversification and Personal Development
    emphasised
Preparation for learning
(Preparation for retirement)

"rep ad fin"

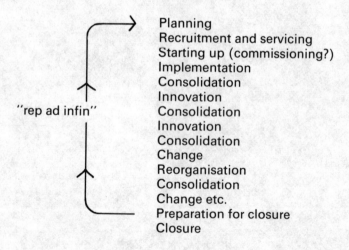

The Organisation

Planning
Recruitment and servicing
Starting up (commissioning?)
Implementation
Consolidation
Innovation
Consolidation
Innovation
Consolidation
Change
Reorganisation
Consolidation
Change etc.
Preparation for closure
Closure

"rep ad infin"

An interesting and useful account of Staff Development is given by Mary Lynn Crow in a report on staff development provision in eleven southern universities in the United States*. She gives nine reasons why the universities themselves were interested in Staff Development in addition to the reason students were interested (it led to better teaching). These reasons are:

Levelling or declining student enrolment
Decreased mobility of faculty and administrators
High percentage of tenured faculty members who were mostly in their forties
A buyer's market for students with regard to educational opportunities
Economic crunch for universities and for students
The need to better equip graduate students to compete for jobs in higher education
The proclivity of students to tell it like it is, not to be awed by a teacher's authority, and to bring legal action if they don't get what they pay for
Increased demand for accountability by parents, board members, legislators and the public in general
An articulate and often negative press.

These reasons provide a picture of educational environment entirely familiar in the United Kingdom situation though some of the pressures (e.g. student recourse to law) are only just beginning to be felt. Above all, the critical factor that forces attention on Staff Development is the immobility of staff, so that frustration builds up for individuals in their own job and the institution because accustomed elasticity has disappeared. Perhaps, however, it is a sad comment on the management of institutions that Staff Development becomes a concern only when the institution is perceived to be threatened. Dr Crow makes a further useful categorisation by drawing on a scheme by Bergquist and Phillips‡ and also one by Gaff‡. The Bergquist and Phillips model consists of the following sections:

---

* "Emphasis on Faculty Development" by Mary Lynn Crow in *"Faculty Development Centres in Southern Universities"* Ed. Mary Lynn Crow et al. Southern Regional Education Board, Atlanta, Georgia. (1976).
† Bergquist, William H. and Phillips, Steven R. *A Handbook for Faculty Development* The Council for the Advancement of Small Colleges. Washington DC 1975.
‡ Gaff Jerry G. "New Approaches to Improve Teaching" in *Learner Centred Reform Current Issues of Higher Education* 1975. Dyckman, W. Vermilye (Ed) Josey Bass San Francisco 1975 pp. 90–97.

135

I. Instructional Development
   A. Evaluation
   B. Diagnosis
   C. Training: Traditional Methods
   D. Training: New Methods and Techniques
   E. Curricular (sic) Development

II. Organisational Development
   A. Team Building
   B. Decision-making
   C. Conflict Management
   D. Problem Solving
   E. Managerial Development

III. Personal Development
   A. Discussions about Teaching
   B. Career – Life Planning
   C. Interpersonal Skills Training
   D. Personal Growth
   E. Therapeutic and Supportive Counselling

Gaff's model is an amplification, in effect, of the Bergquist and Phillips scheme differing only in the terms used to denote personal or individual development.

I. Instructional Development Programmes focus on how the conditions of learning are designed, particularly as these relate to courses. Such programmes strive to improve student learning by such means as preparing learning materials, redesigning courses, and making instruction systematic.

II. Faculty Development programmes focus on the faculty members themselves rather than on the courses they teach. Such programmes strive to promote faculty growth by helping faculty members to acquire knowledge, skills, sensitivity and techniques related to teaching and learning. Areas of emphasis would include knowledge about higher education, feedback about their own teaching behaviour, teacher's affective development, and awareness of other disciplines and the community.

III. Organisational (sic) Development programmes focus on the organisation within which faculty, students and administrators work. This approach strives to develop policies that support teaching improvement and to create an effective environment for teaching and learning by improving interpersonal relationships and enhancing team functioning.

Staff Development relates, as I have already described, to the career of the individual within the organisation and it is clear that the approaches described focus on the needs of the individual within the organisation. But it is not entirely clear how separate Staff Development is from the Personnel function. Recruitment and Conditions of Service, tenure and secondment have technical and legal implications. The recruitment process cannot be separated from induction and the decisions to advertise posts at particular grades depend on decisions about succession planning, organisational needs and even (as is the case just now with universities) the salary level payable – and consequently the experience of new staff. Each institution must work out the differences between Personnel and Welfare on the one hand and Staff Development and Care on the other. One distinction is operational–that between the jobs done by the administrative side of the institution and the academic. Staff Development is largely an academic function and a Staff Development 'Unit' would be staffed essentially by academics.

The size of a Staff Development Unit will depend on the size of the institution but it is unlikely to be less than three academics since the skill areas required are educational technology, curriculum development and instructional design and personal psychology. The likelihood is that Units will begin with staff qualified in the first two discipline areas because they seem to be the most tangible and concrete. In fact, the deepest need is for personal and social psychology because the problems that arise have their basis in problems of personal morale, identity, self-esteem, confidence, fulfilment and so on. With little mobility in educational institutions an increasing and large number of Staff Development problems will be concerned with individual dilemmas. One can predict with some certainty that staff problems in the next decade will be concerned with personal satisfaction at work and at home, boredom, frustration, fear and anxiety about the future, and emotional withdrawal as a consequence of aging and maturing. Equally, more and more students will be adult on part-time or shortened courses who are facing the same personal problems as their tutors.

In addition, to the traditional "training" methods used in initial teacher training, industrial training departments and even, until quite recently advocated by the University Teaching Methods Unit*, new approaches will have to be found that focus on personal needs rather than technical skills. Though technical skills training is essential for

---

* See for instance, "Improving Teaching in Higher Education" UTMU 55 Gordon Square, London, 1976 Some small change is offered in the courses offered for January-June 1978 evidenced by more emphasis on understanding the experience of learning in groups.

137

some types of teaching it is a basic necessity and not a consequential necessity. Even when teachers are fully able to do all that teaching requires of them, they will have a large area of problems. Indeed, I suspect this is by far the largest area of problem. New forms of job enrichment, staff secondment, day release and partial employment will have to be thought of. Even the current vogue of giving a year off for work towards a higher degree is unsatisfactory because it no longer leads almost automatically to promotion and the staff member returns needing to come into a more richly rewarded situation. And, from an organisational point of view, few departments really know how to use the potential and undeveloped skills of staff. The blockages to creativity in organisations, especially (surprisingly enough) educational ones, can be quite horrendous.

The details of how a Staff Development Unit works must inevitably depend on the leadership of the institution. It can be a key element in institutional development or a backwater for awkward staff. Success will only come if the Unit has high organisational status, the members are highly regarded academically by their professional colleagues and if they work collaboratively with staff, units and departments. Staff Development Units fulfil a facilitative role at every juncture and are not an instrument of management coercion. Hence staff must practice a great deal of tact in personal relationships while engaging in visible and recognised work. Unit staff should also have temporary membership (four or five years) so that the Unit is seen to reflect the developments of the institution enacted by the staff as a whole and not by a specialised clique. That is not to say that Unit staff should always return to their home department. It would be a greater evidence of true development if they were seen to move to a new sphere of activity. The Head of the Unit may be a permanent member because he must have high status comparable with most of the senior executive staff of the institution (e.g. Head of Department or Dean). But since one organisational form of change is to pay promoted salaries to individuals without linking them to organisational status, there is no reason why a Head of Unit on a Head of Department salary should not fulfil a simple teaching role, nor is there any reason why an 'ordinary' teacher should not act as a chairman of a department for a year or so.

The only way in which educational institutions can develop to cope with the future is by taking the emphasis away from course development and towards staff development. That is because the nature of courses depends on the kind of people who design them. Until people are helped to change without fear, they cannot commit themselves to organisational change.

138

11.
Staff Counselling in Education†

† *Appeared in J. or Further and in the education Vol. 3 No. 1 Spring 1979.*

There has been a considerable increase in recent years in interest in Staff Development in Higher Education. For the most part this has been concerned with improving the quality of teaching, increasing the opportunities for further professional development, and introducing the idea of management training or development for senior staff of Further and Higher education institutions. A useful account of developments in the university context is given in the Changing University where the term Staff Development is preferred for the activity of further professional training in the organisational context. Staff Development is defined as:

"a systematic attempt to harmonize individual's interests and wishes and their carefully assessed requirements for furthering their careers with the forthcoming requirements of the organisation within which they expected (sic) to work".*

It is virtually inevitable that Staff Development programmes take on an institutional form and become an additional dimension of management and control and it is not unlikely that as Staff Development catches on, as it surely will, it becomes a somewhat mechanical and authoritarian process — a tendency hinted in the quotation given.

One aspect of Staff Development, however, which has not received much attention and is perhaps less open to manipulation is Staff Counselling. Staff Development usually manifests itself in some form of course or collective event outside the organisation or marginal to its central activity.‡ Hardly anyone takes Staff Development seriously apart from the individual who wants time off to attend a course or conference in which he is interested or who wants secondment or sabbatical leave to obtain a higher qualification or to do some research and teaching elsewhere. There are good reasons for being cynical about Staff Development as at present practised but no useful purpose will be served here by rehearsing what is well known among further and higher education teachers. There are other positive things to be said.

In schools, colleges, universities and polytechnics there has grown up over the years a considerable provision in student counselling, often of a very high order and, by now, very well known. More recently the concern for student welfare has extended the idea of counselling to a more general one of 'pastoral care'.§ In institutions of Further and Higher education provision of student services is often of a high order although there is a great deal still to be done. However, the logical

---

* David Warren Piper and Ron Glatter: The Changing University NFER 1977 p. 24.
‡ In spite of a contary implication in Ron Glatter's grid (p. 26) op. cit.
§ Best R. E., Jarvis C. B., Ribbins P. M., Pastoral Care: Concept and Process. British Journal of Educational Studies Vol. XXV No. 2 June 1977.

extension of concern to a pastoral concern for staff does not seem to have been made and in this regard educational institutions are more lacking than almost any other form of adult employment. There has always been a strong, and doubtless valuable, tradition that teachers are well able to look after themselves and do not need the 'care' that it is generally considered other groups of employees require. Yet in some regards teachers are more at risk than other groups – doctors and lawyers, perhaps, only excepted.

There is a great deal of observational evidence, currently highlighted in the closing of colleges of education, that the general pastoral care of teaching staff is largely neglected. Teachers might well be reluctant to demand the kind of provision that outsiders would consider essential and, indeed, there was considerable reaction within education at the introduction of a 'personnel function' at the time of local government reorganisation. Even where the promise of help (or interference) from Local Government Personnel Departments was made, nothing of any consequence followed. Yet it would seem that an essential area of development within present resources is one of pastoral concern within schools, colleges, polytechnics and universities and that the initial emphasis should be on the most pressing need which is not so much for Staff Development as forms of personal counselling.

Anyone with experience of education knows that most problems of individuals have a very personal nature. There is no collective tradition in education as there is elsewhere, especially in industry, where the role of shop steward is important. Nor do teachers have interviews with their bosses over organisational matters in the way that other workers do – negotiating pay rises, holiday dates, leave of absence, production or equipment problems, working conditions. Teachers tend to accept very readily the cicumstances in which they find themselves and do not expect their boss to change them overnight. Teachers grumble among themselves – often loud and long enough but still among themselves – and keep personal matters out of the conversation. In many ways it behoves a teacher to be seen to be just like other workers. As a consequence, problems become personalised and are often kept secret when they should be shared. The answer to the situation is the development of personal counselling within the institution by specially trained staff who have the status to deal easily and comfortably with the senior management team; the same relationship to the institution as Student Counsellors but distinct from Student Services. The Staff Counselling Group would most appropriately be members of the institution's Staff Development Unit but would have this additional professional function. The kind of matters that would receive their attention can be described in general terms and fall into three categories

142

— organisational matters, career and professional issues, and personal problems.

Organisational matters arise when there is some conflict or puzzle-ment between the individual and the organisation. They may be issues of relationship with superiors or subordinates or members of the administration. A teacher often experiences exasperation and/or frustration but because of the way the system works he will be unable to resolve the matter. So frustration and anger build up in his mind and he needs help to unravel the feelings that have engulfed him. The incidence of organisational anxiety is much greater than senior staff ever acknowledge for they often have no idea of the state of morale of their colleagues or the aggression that is hidden for the sake of propriety or a political sense. These problems are ones we commonly expect from members of any organisation but just because they are common they are no less important. Sometimes we tend to be impatient but however reasonable or otherwise the outsider may consider a problem to be, to the one who faces the problem matters can be difficult enough. Just as Heads of Department have 'subordinate' colleagues who present difficulties, so subordinates have problems with their Heads. In educational institutions not nearly enough recognition is given to problems of relationships. Yet all the prognostications are that inter-personal problems will increase as promotion prospects deteriorate and there becomes less mobility in the educational system. Then there are problems of role, role definition and role expectation which are exaggerated in education where role behaviour is never well defined but expectations are often considerable, severe and not well negotiated. Counselling helps to sort matters out.

A second group of organisational problems centres around problems with students. It is not easy for teachers to be aware of the difficulties of students until they are suddenly surprised when something has gone badly wrong. It may then be easy enough to call in help for the student from Student Services but the teacher himself needs help and reassurance. This is especially so when students have breakdowns or threaten desperate behaviour or attempt suicide, or are in financial, marital or health difficulties. Often the teacher does not know how to respond, or whether he has taken the right action. He may not know whether to call in help or not; or even what help is available. Sometimes he spends many hours with the student trying ineffectively to 'counsel' but because he has few skills he makes the matters worse, at least for himself. Teachers need support quite frequently in such situations and only an acceptable and available colleague who can be a personal counsellor will help him through a period of considerable stress. Further-more, when a teacher knows that he, too, can go to a trained counsellor for advice, the speed with which help is provided for the student is increased.

Teachers often worry needlessly about the problems of students. Sometimes this arises out of a real sympathy and concern but sometimes it is because of needs in the teacher himself. Teachers need to feel successful and yet there are few occasions when they receive the affirming strokes they need. When a student asks for attention he is showing his need for his teacher and the opportunity to be actively wanted is often too good to miss. Usually there is little awareness of this mutuality of need but just as in psychotherapy it is recognised that the psychotherapist often needs his client as much as vice versa, so it is with teachers and students. When counselling help is available, the teacher can more easily direct his energies towards student needs instead of also working, albeit subconciously, on his own needs. And counsellors can provide in a realistic way the emotional support and affirmation the teacher requires.

The career problems of teachers are largely overlooked in all kinds of educational institutions. For a long time it was considered indecent to express openly one's ambition and even nowadays there is a coyness about promotion that is quite unrealistic. Promotion for any teacher is a token of recognition and few educational institutions offer other forms of recognition. Indeed, in Higher Education, external recognition of the teacher is demanded – publications, reviews, outside lectureships and consultancy – before the institution is prepared to show recognition. And often the institution is not prepared to support requests for time and consideration to gain outside recognition. It is often thought that advantages occur to awkward and difficult members of staff because they are the only ones seen to benefit from manoeuvring in jobs and perquisites. Organisations need to find other ways of rewarding people but many problems are less concerned with monetary reward than other kinds of recognition. Counselling can help individuals, especially those in mid and late career, to come to see their present position much more clearly and positively and to be aware of the potential advantages. At the same time, good counselling will help in the making of a correct appraisal of the situation, a realistic acknowlegement of a bad situation and the development of strategies to deal with it.

It should be quite possible to design six-monthly appraisal sessions based on a form of counselling in which colleagues examine together their current professional and personal situations. The older type of appraisal based on industrial management by objectives models is not suited to educational organisations. The idea of setting quantifiable targets is foreign to the work of education and against the climate of most schools and colleges. But there are kinds of targets or objectives

144

expressed in a general way that are meaningful to teachers and these can be developed in discussion. Counselling appraisal is non-hierarchical but is an opportunity to talk through with one or two colleagues (perhaps with the help of one as a third party facilitator) how a teacher feels about himself and his job at the present time and how he plans to develop things in the future. In this form of appraisal, the only promises he makes are to himself and they become both realistic and challenging but not potentially condemnatory.

Other career decisions may be more critical and techniques from occupational psychology may be employed by counsellors. We are moving into a period where there may be more changes in jobs, in mid-career, more early retirements, more changing direction. It seems ridiculous for an individual to occupy the same job or even the same type of job for 30 years or more. The whole concept of full-time employment needs to come into question and there are many possibilities for enrichment of occupation within employment. Education, of all types of employment, ought to be able to offer the richest range of alternative and additional activities. We have hardly begun to think about new ways of organising education and exploring the possibilities of an enriched quality of employment. Yet this is an area that will increasingly concern us. Earlier retirement should not be a new and deadly phase of employment but a fulfilment of opportunities and activities developed during the earlier years. Good counselling helps an individual to see his work in perspective and to look for opportunities of life enrichment that are not dependent on acknowledged "success" in his job.

There is an important continuing area of pastoral concern in the whole institutional professional life of each teacher. The administrative elements in his job from induction to retirement are all concerns for pastoral care and counselling help. There are the stages of induction, settling in, seeking promotion, mid-career, settling down to the late career, security (or otherwise) and pre-retirement. Many teachers need to make careful appraisal in their first year of teaching and others will do so at other crucial times. Induction is a very personal matter as well as an institutional one. We make too many assumptions about the way people fit into organisations; we take unilateral decisions on behalf of our colleagues. Teaching problems do not all occur in the first year and it is more difficult to admit them later on. Many issues subsumed under further training or staff development are essentially personal. Managerial competence and qualities of leadership are more likely to be dependent on the self-concept and personality adjustment than technical issues. Good leadership and good management cannot be taught as skills and techniques, they are qualities of personality –

confidence, self security, realistic self-awareness, empathy. Problems of inter-personal relations more often than not require counselling rather than training of individuals in techniques.

There is little doubt that much of the effort put into training for leadership, for instance, is misplaced. Leadership style is a function of personality not a theatrical part that can be learned. The critical area for leadership in educational institutions is Head of Department or Unit. Many leaders need to change their style of behaviour if they are to become more effective because the qualities that brought them to their position are seldom the ones they need in a 'management' role. Yet to have to change one's behaviour is the most threatening requirement of all and no 'training' can bring it about. Only a counselling mode can build the self-confidence necessary in changed behaviour, a significant change in the self-concept and in the individual's view of his position in the world. Sadly, the managers who need the most help are the least likely to ask for it.

The third group of problems is "personal" in that they originate outside the institution. It is generally recognised that we do not live in separate worlds but bring the same personal qualities to all situations. Whether each new situation is congenial or not is a matter for discovery. A teacher may be happy at work and unhappy at home because of factors in each situation. But generally we carry much with us from situation to situation. Marriage problems affect our relationships and preoccupations at work. Health certainly affects us everywhere though some situations may be easier than others. Each of us brings a whole range of personal problems to work and many of them get in the way of our relationships and performance. All of us can use some help; some of us need a great deal. It can be provided by a good, comprehensive counselling provision because the confidentiality of shared experience is assured. Indeed, it may be much easier to seek professional counselling help at work than to go and seek it from some external agency.

One approach to counselling that has been attempted* is to develop counselling as a mode of operation throughout the institution — to consider counselling as a basis for all relationships, teaching and managerial. Counselling training is offered to all staff (teaching and administrative) who wish and an initial programme is followed by further counselling training sessions and case consultancy. The idea is

---

* At the Anglian Regional Management Centre, N.E. London Polytechnic, during 1976–77 a programme of counselling training was introduced to staff who were interested. Nearly half the academic staff attended.

146

to move into a facilitative and caring climate of organisation and to move away from the normal hierarchic dependency situation. A great deal of time is required for this shift in organisational climate but it is the only way in which an educational process can be truly collaborative between teachers and students, as well as teachers themselves. Since so much of what passes for education is denied in the educational process itself, the challenge of change for educational institutions is initially critical. Counselling skills are available. Many teachers are familiar with their use; a comparative few are trained in some way as counsellors and a shift towards a wide counselling mode in colleges etc. should now be possible.

It certainly cannot be denied that the need for more pastoral concern for teaching and administrative staff in education is long overdue. Many problems in educational reform arise because teachers are emotionally unsupported and fear change. The demands on education to change and adapt will become greater not less in the next decade or so and the long neglected area of staff relationships needs immediate attention. Throughout its history, reform has overlooked the personal needs of the teachers. In a counselling mode, the balance of attention to the intellectual and emotional sides of personality receives a correct and stabilised equilibrium. For too long it has been assumed that only the intellects of teachers require development and many have become emotionally under-nourished as a consequence. This missing dimension must be brought back into educational organisation for it is strange how the concern for students by teachers has not extended to teachers themselves. After all, it was teachers themselves who developed the concept and skills of systematic pastoral care and it would be a sad irony if they were to suffer by neglecting to employ counselling for their own needs.

12.
Planning and the Curriculum

The primary purpose of an educational institution is the provision and organisation of an educational process for the members. Concerned in this primary purpose are the primary members – those around whom the essential teaching/learning process revolves. The curriculum is the content of the process in which these primary members are involved. We are accustomed to speak of teachers, students and pupils, and to describe the curriculum in term of subjects. But if we are properly to understand the planning and decision making structure of an educational institution we need to be much clearer than is generally the case about the nature of membership, the nature of curriculum and the ways in which change and innovation come about. Currently 'rational' approaches to educational planning are still commonly held although they do not deal with basic questions about the nature of academic institutions and they generally ignore the psychology of institutional decision making.

We may define curriculum simply as the primary educational activity of the institution*. Curriculum is the organised activity of the institution but also includes a good deal of what is informal. We can see the contrast at its greatest between the infant school and the polytechnic or university. In the primary school, it is customary to consider almost every activity as educational – taking off hats and coats and hanging them up, learning to do up shoe laces, playing with clay, learning about numbers and listening to stories. In the polytechnic there is a clear division between formal activity and informal and only the formal, expressed in terms of subjects or courses, is measured and even valued. In the infant school, learning and living is integrated but in the polytechnic the official emphasis is on cognition and the acquisition of specific skills. In between there is a progression towards specialisation which leads to an unresolved dichotomy between that which is valued highly (competence in subjects) and that which is valued much less (mere survival in the system). The two most obvious features of the education system as we move from first school to university are selection and alienation. Educational systems always appear to tend towards differentiation in terms of educational content and to invest most highly in certain selected groups. Such differentiation tends also to be elitist though differentiation and selection are not in themselves elitist. Elitism occurs only when certain value judgements are made about what is selected and what is rejected.

Secondary education institutions are unable satisfactorily to deal with the problems of selection, differentiation and dichotomy. Post-

---

* See also Becher T., & Maclure S., 'The Politics of Curriculum Change' (especially Chapter I) Hutchinson 1978.

secondary institutions deal with the problems by discounting and excluding those educational activities which they do not want or cannot cope with. Often they choose to deal with only those activities that have high social prestige. Thereafter, there is a historical force to continue with traditional programmes. When we examine an institution of higher education we see that the educational process is expressed almost solely in terms of academic 'subjects' and the organisation of subjects occurs in terms of a time-table. Secondary schools are even more dominated by time-tables because they are places where teachers are considered to be responsible for supervising the whole of the time children are at school. Further and Higher Education is concerned with students only to the extent that they lead to the provision of programmes and courses made up of subjects. Outside hours allocated to subjects, the Higher and Further Education institution has little responsibility for students. Apart from some eccentric experiments*, developments in Higher Education occur in terms of traditional subjects rather than for 'educational' reasons. The few attempts at modular provision (City of London Polytechnic or Bristol Polytechnic for instance) are subject rather than "education" based, even though they were intended to open up possibilities for an education rather than mere subject provision.

In the primary school, there is an intimate involvement between the teacher and the child, between the teacher and groups of children. This involvement is not confined to, or even essentially, a cerebral (intellectual) relationship; it is an emotional, whole person to whole person relationship. In secondary schools, this intimacy is regretted and so systems of pastoral care arise to compensate for what has been lost. In Further and Higher Education this relationship initially disappears. In schools the impetus to develop the educational process comes from within the teaching profession; innovation tends to arise out of an awareness of need on the part of the teachers. There are signs that this may change a little as there is a public criticism of the fruits of education – a generally misinformed criticism often emanating from industrialists who will not face their own educational responsibilities. In Higher Education, the need for the relevance of education has been more diffuse but external demands have generally been taken note of. The focus of attention in schools has been domestic and internal while the focus of Higher Education – especially the polytechnics – has been on employment, the employability of students. So long as students can obtain jobs, it is considered that courses meet needs. In addition, there

---

* *Perhaps the Keele Foundation year and the Keele concept of a residential university.*

152

has always been something of an entrepreneurial spirit in Higher and Further Education which has often seemed like doctors asking patients what illnesses they would like to suffer from and then setting themselves up as pharmacists in preference to physicians.

No one doubts that elementary (primary) education should be the education of the whole child but after this stage the demand seems to become increasingly for automata with excellent skills and no minds of their own. Many Employers for instance, cannot really want people who think for themselves for such people will not easily accept what employers want them to do. Whenever we consider the provision of Higher Education we are faced with the dilemma that the better the education, the more frustrated will be the student. Once he leaves College the provision of courses in polytechnics etc., must be seen against this contradiction; if courses develop to meet demand they will cease to be educational and become increasingly frustrating to students. That we all have to experience a large amount of frustration at work is no excuse for ignoring the personal needs of students as against the supposed professional needs. The better we teach a subject the less well prepared the student may be to use it for the normal requirements of industry and commerce.

It may be argued that as the student passes through the stages of education, he becomes increasingly responsible for exercising choices in his own learning. In secondary schools, choices are offered (or required) in about the third and fourth years. The effect of these choices is to influence the employment options of the student in some way. Children of 13 and 14 may or may not be mature enough to exercise subject choices but even if they make choices valid in every respect at that age, these choices cannot remain valid for the rest of the indivual's life except, perhaps, in the rarest of cases. An educational system must make provision for further changes that will minimize the effect of previous choice so far as that is possible. A system of training or instruction that commits a student to a single lifetime choice can only exist in a totally static social economy – and there is no such thing. No educational system can survive that produces only people trained for only one small employment slot; this caution must be born very much in mind when talk is made about schools and colleges not producing the students industry and commerce require – an issue that will be fought hard in the nineteen eighties and nineties.

The Further Education tradition – which is remarkably strong in Higher Education just now in an unexpected way because of the failure of the polytechnics to reform Higher Education – has grown up in the tradition of training for employment. That is, of training for employment in prescribed slots. The problem of relating manpower planning to

153

education is that the discussion changes from education to training. The danger for the Manpower Services Commission is that it will be concerned with training and not education. Such an influence may or may not be pernicious but there is evidence that work experience schemes are successful because they make young school leavers more employable by being acculturated into industrial norms. If the consequence be a demand that schools should perform this socialisation process then education is indeed in danger.

The pressure on the schools to train for industry may well increase. The same pressure in Further Education colleges will always exist for the under 25's because of the various forms of (quota) pressures by Regional Advisory Councils, Professional Institutes and local employment conditions. And it would be disastrous for Further Education to ignore the realities of the employment situation; the history of the computer industry is an object lesson to everyone. The problem for the polytechnics is that they overlap in the kind of professional provision they make with the colleges of Further Education and are more subject to consumer demand than the universities hence the tendency of the polytechnics is to look towards fulfilling industrial need in terms of course (subject and skill) content rather than in the intellectual resilience of students. Close relationship to employment need is a double bind because unless the polytechnics fulfil needs in the present they do not survive yet their future becomes at risk because they have not anticipated the future. Engineering is usually quoted as an example of this but a second paradox is that those subject departments that are most comfortable at the present moment because they have a plentiful supply of students doing traditional courses are most at risk because they have no energy or resources to spare to look to the future. We need to discover how programmes change, how they meet needs and how they change to meet future needs, and we have to be a good deal clearer about the relationship between education and training.

We have just passed through a decade or more of change in primary and secondary education. Acres of paper have been covered with accounts of these changes in the United Kingdom and abroad but no one appears to be much wiser about how curriculum change occurs other than as a manifestation of a more general social change. The 1950's and 1960's were a period of general educational 'reform' seen most clearly in the move to comprehensive secondary schools and open education in the primary school. The reform movement has yet to reach post-secondary education though there are indications as to how it will go*. Reform arises out of a generalised social response to economic

---

* In the general idea of Recurrent Education, perhaps and the Open College.

154

changes; hence the open plan primary school in the U.K., was a response to ease pressure on the schools caused by a period of an expanding economy and full employment. The retraction in education reform coincides fairly well with an economic recession. Further Education is more vulnerable to economic factors than any other sector of education and this reflects most immediately in the content of courses taught.

Curriculum change in the primary and secondary school (and for different reasons in the university) is brought about within the schools themselves, by the teachers. The open plan primary school was a teachers' revolution and was not brought about by parents, employers or industrial demand. Likewise, the reforms in secondary education in the School Certificate, which became the General Certificate of Education, and the Certificate of Secondary Education. Change in the curriculum content was made by teachers themselves working on new subjects, new syllabuses and new methods. On the other hand, reforms in Further Education are imposed from without— and then are dubiously termed 'reforms' — for example TEC and BEC and all the professional institute examinations. It is almost impossible to bring about an educational reform in higher education, only a change in training techniques. The one exception has been the Dip.HE and that arose from a particular situation, largely internal to education itself, the reorganisation of teacher training (or teacher education).*

It is likely that increased pressure will be brought on schools to revert to training — at least in the sense of the 1870 Education Act with its concern to equip the working classes with the basic skills necessary for an expanding industrial economy. Changes in the membership of the Schools Council to include a dominance by non-teachers suggest such pressures and the discussion around the 'N' and 'F' school leaving certificate may well reflect this external concern. This interest is almost solely economic and to do with employability of young people at the expense of the vaster area of social and economic reform needed in a society that is becoming more divided by race and class and more at risk in terms of social order and cohesiveness. The semi-political nature of 'reform' pressures as usual avoids the real issues as the effort goes into the protection of wealth and property. Such an interpretation is not marxist but, hopefully, self-evident if one is to observe the topics of concern in the daily press and on the radio.

The period of greatest confidence in the planning process culminated

---

* The 'James' Report and the subsequent government White Paper.

in the reorganisation of Local Government in the early 1970's and was epitomised by the reorganisation of the Hospital Service. Since then confidence in planning has been severely eroded. In education the calamity was at its most extreme with the sudden dismantling of the teacher training system in the mid 1970's though there are those who claim that the writing on the wall was there for everyone to see. Though the local authorities went on blithely building new colleges of education while their own birth rates were falling, the fact is that the closure of colleges of education was very badly bungled and no one has accepted responsibility for the chaos. Yet the demise of the colleges of education should come as no surprise; social events always occur in this way, always catch everyone unawares but for a few pundits hidden away in the undergrowth. Pearl Harbour was one example, the next atomic war will be another.

Planning processes do not deal with the future, they are little more than extrapolations about (not 'from') the present. People just do not prepare for the future in economic terms at all* except for those who keep a well stocked larder and deep freeze. The reasons for this is that we can never know from what source an irresistible demand will come. We can only guess in terms of what we now know – but the fact that we know it now means that we have contained it. The colleges of education need never have been closed if someone had decided on a use for them. It was quite possible for the Department of Education and Science to have ordained that there would be an expansion of adult education, or work-experience, to take in the colleges. If the necessary financial provision had been made then such a change could have been brought about. Such a development would not be a matter for planning at all, simply the exercise of power by an individual in the position to exercise that power. Social change is more commonly brought about by arbitrary fiat than by planning. On the other hand, there are two important resources available in any social situation, these are access to currently valid data and the emotional condition conductive to change in the organisation.

The availability of information to the institution – that is, usually available – is a critical factor in response to threatened change. Arguments are made not on the basis of truly objective information but on subjectively selected information. It is the persuasiveness of subjectivity that is critical since persuasion involves the affective level of

* *Perhaps the classic critique of planning processes is in Charles E. Lindblom, "The Science of Muddling Through", Public Administration Review Vol. 19 (1959). Its comparatively early date is worth noting.*

response, itself more potent than the purely cerebral level. Solely subjective opinions may or may not be influential but they must have an appearance of quantifiability in them. For a polytechnic to be able to quote a local unemployment rate of 12 % is of itself an argument for nothing. For it to quote a 12 % unemployment rate of men and women with an expressed interest in part-time education is more persuasive. Demographic data is useful only if used not to make projections but to respond to situations that have already arisen. And, of course, once a polytechnic or college begins to deal in current rather than future data, the need to respond currently becomes more urgent.

The second factor in responding to threat or opportunity is the current state of responsiveness to change. Most educational institutions are responding to the change pressures of from five to ten years ago, perhaps more. Generally speaking institutions respond to past situations not present ones. They set up permanent structures like degree courses that stretch interminably into the future and take up resources in anticipation. Such institutions are characterised by a small number of 'outriders' or entrepreneurs who keep bringing their interpretations of the future into the organisation and encouraging more central members to change according to these "identified needs". As soon as the central members have begun to respond, the peripheral men come in again with another new idea, maybe in contradiction to their last one. That is how most institutions work—on this "centre-periphery" model in which rewards tend to go to the innovator even though he does little more in fact than float the idea and is then off looking for another. An organisational change is required that involves only short term 'planning' (e.g. courses only planned for three years on the understanding that they will be radically changed whatever happens at the end of the third year; and the personnel involved will be changed). And the flow of staff between the centre and the periphery will be maintained on a related cycle (e.g. course changes of three years means staff changes every four to five years). Thus staff changes will occur throughout the system and to all levels and as a consequence the nature of programmes will change too.

There is a critical reason for locating the source of change in individuals. In the end, only an individual can respond to change — organisations cannot change. Furthermore, change is an emotional/intellectual process deriving from an individual's response to his environment. While we all respond differently to the same situation and some respond more creatively than others, there is less chance of change the less the individual is subjected to change. There is always a response to changed circumstances and any change, however slight, gives greater freedom to those consciously wishing to bring about

157

change. (For this reason alone, "change for the sake of change" is a better maxim than "no change without necessity").

The essential conditions, then, in which change will occur are movement and flexibility in the organisation and the availability of relevant data (material and demographic) to all the members. Of course, there are some circumstances where there is so much movement of members that all the energy is taken up in coping with the movement. That is a common enough phenomenon in education particularly in merger situations where little positive work is done because all the effort is directed to obtaining personal security. Personal security is important, of course, but the amount of security necessary for personal motivation varies from individual to individual. Within organisations individuals obtain security more from recognition by colleagues and superiors than security of tenure of their position, but the almost universal tendency of educational institutions is to express an evaluation of a member in terms of promotion or failure to promote. And the essential condition for promotion is that behaviour should be compatible with the needs of senior staff (or, more cynically, senior staff reward those who do what they are told). Because educational institutions reward for comformity and biddability, they lose a great deal of the energy that could go into the change dynamic of the organisation. Individuals put energy into their job in order to obtain promotion but almost invariably promotion for the most creative members is to a position outside the organisation. Those who are promoted internally tend to be traditional and conformist — and it takes only a moment's reflection to see why this must be so. Institutions need to lose members if they are in a healthy state of response to change and on the whole the most creative people are the ones most able to find jobs elsewhere. Whether this will remain so in a period of contraction is open to question, however. Furthermore, creative members put their colleagues under pressure and strain that they often cannot cope with so that it is organisationally necessary for the high-fliers to move on while the others regain their equilibrium. If, however, there is a good deal of movement within the organisation, creative members can be moved about to discover new niches in old corners. The danger is that they are merely shunted into quiet corners.

Because of the way in which Further Education and Higher Education courses are organised, changes in syllabus and curriculum tend to be sudden and considerable. There is much heart searching about the new methods and breast beating at the loss of old and prized contents. Fossilisation of the curriculum is what has happened. Yet if institutions are themselves in an environment of constant change, so must be the whole educational process and its content. There would seem to be no good reason why syllabus content cannot be under constant revision (most teachers would argue that some change actually happens though the significant change is little enough on close examination). Organic and dynamic change occurs in the content only when either (or both) teachers continually change and/or there is a deliberate concern with the revision of the syllabus in accord with subject awareness rather than market demand. Market demand is the spectre of FE curriculum change. There is no such thing as 'market demand' as distinct from subject change. An electrical engineer who knows his subject will change his course in advance of "market demand" because he knows that the market will change because of new developments in the 'subject'. One may call this an issue of professional integrity; that many FE staff do not have this profesional integrity is a sad reality and a reason for the further professional training of staff as a constant, continuous process. Staff Development is the *sine quo non* of educational change and innovation.

We need to be clear about how innovation actually commences. All discussion about innovation must perforce be reflective because there is no means of anticipating an innovation. We recognise an innovation only when it has occurred. At any given time there are a lot of new ideas in the air. Some of these ideas are 'of their time' and some are not. The history of scientific invention and discovery shows clearly the adoption of ideas only in the fullness of their time. Educators are equally familiar with ideas that are shared by people who until a certain moment had never met and writers are frequently surprised that what they believed were their own ideas are commonly shared with others who appear also to have thought of the same things spontaneously. So there are always a lot of ideas current, many more than can be dealt with. Individuals when involved tend to react against situations rather than respond to them. By this is meant that change by definition is a reaction against something that is already going on*. Reform occurs at the instance of those concerned in the activity rather than those outside it — since how else can one relate to a circumstance. Reform begins in a mental reaction against a situation that is already well advanced and developed. That is the starting point of all change, when one begins to look for alternatives. These alternatives are tested for practicability and/or reality (that is, they may be preferable but impossible or unacceptable even though necessary). Once an alternative becomes attractive all sorts of support are looked for with a preference for support rather than criticism. Most support will be a rationalisation of the evidence however good the case

---

* It must be doubtful if change can ever be 'proactive'. There is a good deal of wishful thinking about proactive behaviour in education.

159

for reform because no reform can be validated until after it has been tried.

There are certain personal conditions for the adoption of an innovative idea. They have a great deal to do with personality and much to do with the circumstances of the individual in the organisation. An individual must believe himself to have energy resources for the innovation and for the change to be in his interests, personally or institutionally. Innovation is not adopted without motivation and motivation is an aspect of self-interest. Innovation depends on the ability of the initiating individual to persuade others in the organisation that the proposed innovation will also be in their self interest. This will be so if they, too, feel that they have spare energy to cope with those organisational effects of the innovation that will concern them. We may say that any individual in an organisation will be somewhere on a continuum from high motivation to low motivation though the reasons for each person will be different. Very little is known about innovatory persons* but we can guess at the organisational conditions necessary for the innovator to be active. (Most accounts of innovation are fantasy reconstructions of events rather than analyses of the process at the social, psychological and truly political levels)†.

There are three levels of innovation within an organisation. Organisational, group or departmental, and individual. The individual level is where an individual changes the style of his teaching, the content of the syllabus and/or introduces new practices e.g. field studies, group essays and so on. Individual innovation can take place without reference to others and may be described as personal style of teaching. It is possible without sanctions from other people in the organisation. All the risks are taken by the individual alone.

The Departmental or group level is where a number of individuals are involved in a subject, course or programme (they may or may not work as a team) and where agreement is required because several groups of students may be involved as well as more than one teacher. Again, changes in syllabus, teaching method, field studies and external visits, mode of examining may be involved. The key factor here is the relationship among the members of the group etc., and their collective relationship with the leader or departmental head. The burden of risk-

---

* *There is a growing literature on industrial innovation and the concept of the entrepreneur. An interesting application of the concept to education is in my "The Entrepreneurial Innovator" in Management Education and Development, Vol. 9, Part 2, Aug. 1978.*

† *See Per Dalin: Case Studies of Educational Innovation OECD 1973. This is a classic account of educational innovation.*

taking is shared but there is an added responsibility that falls to the head because he is middle-man between his group members and the (collective) 'leadership' of the institution.

The organisational or institutional level is the most political and innovation depends on the attitude and disposition of the institutional head. Almost everything depends on his personal disposition (personality, character) and the way he perceives his position in political terms vis à vis the employing authority, governors or managers, and the national situation as he relates it to his institution. Some institution heads believe in leadership by coercion while others see leadership as being a function of facilitating what others want to do. The behaviour of the institutional leader is by far and away the most critical in terms of morale in the institution but at institutional level the game is one of gaining a high reputation for the institution and obtaining greater resources for the institution. The self-interest of the leader may or may not be incompatible with the self-interest of members but that depends on how rewards and punishments are awarded and the extent to which the interests of people are given preference over institutional interests. There is a tendency for leaders to objectify their own personal interests into institutional interests as a way of bludgeoning colleagues into acceptance and submission. At the institutional level of innovation, data is simply an instrument for bargaining and its intrinsic veracity is not very important. Decisions are made not in terms of data but in terms of people (that is, in terms of the influence of preferred individuals). However, once a decision has been made at institutional level it will be made to work because (1) resources will be made available and (2) it will be shown to work even if the eventual content is quite different from that intended*.

Invariably, data will be provided in support of a curriculum change after the idea of that curriculum change has taken root. It is virtually impossible for anyone in an educational institution to look at demographic data first of all and translate that into curriculum requirements. The more usual course of events is for an individual to feel and perceive a need because of some personal experience (e.g. teaching Cypriot children) and looking for evidence of the extent of the problem(s) he identifies. More common in curriculum terms, an individual teacher thinks up a new 'combination' expresses this as a new curriculum concept e.g. related studies, practical arts, and then looks for justification for teaching this new subject. The innovation

---

* *For instance, in many colleges there would be no difficulty in changing the Dip.HE courses to the first two years of a normal Bachelors degree if that were the only way to attract students and funds.*

begins when he starts to marshal arguments in favour of the new subject.

Primary and secondary schools have more flexibility in their content than Further and Higher Education because the organisational implications are potentially fewer. More people are generally concerned in deciding the content of a course at Further and Higher level – a professional panel, a 'national' qualification, an 'institute' requirement. Universities and polytechnics tend not to implement the changes that are potentially theirs because of the force of tradition. New courses are offered as alternatives or additions rather than as integral parts of a change. In schools changes, (largely, small changes) can be integrated more easily. The reasons for this situation also have to do with the control of the time-table. The primary school time-table is exceedingly flexible; the second school time-table is open to manipulation but the Further Education time-table tends to be rigid because it is organised around a huge range of administrative considerations. In Further Education the demands of part-time courses for time allocation may be a first call in time-table considerations. The remarkable apparent difference between schools and colleges is the free time available outside the time-tabled lectures. Yet this 'free' time is often taken up with any number of committees, tutorials, administrative matters and preparation (and sometimes research). The effect of this is for innovation in Further and Higher Education to be viewed as a much more major activity than in schools but because this would require more time commitment there is often a reluctance to initiate. It is also likely that FE teachers are less confident about their subject areas than primary and secondary teachers because they are teaching a more sensitive group of clients.

We may consider the process for curriculum innovation to follow a characteristic pattern. To begin with there is a felt need by an individual which he shares with others. As he gathers support – or in order to gather support – he will write up a proposition which undergoes modification and discussion. When the proposition is in a persuasive form it will be formally adopted in some way particular to the organisation. At this point, a decision is made about the allocation of resources to the programme (staff, money, students, time-table time, accommodation). Often this last decision is not made until external approval has been given if such is required. The critical stage of the innovation is the period when the proposition is formalised in some report or tentative submission (e.g. to GCE Board or CNAA). Once it appears likely that the innovation will be officially accepted, other members of the institution line up in support or otherwise of the project; views will depend on whether the innovation is seen as favoured or otherwise by the senior management group. The whole process becomes part of the political activity of the institution though how serious political issues are will depend on the general climate of the organisation. Large organisations are by their very nature more political than small ones. The crucial factor in the process is the time when resources are actually promised in detail to the implementation of the project.

Curriculum organisation, expressed in terms of time-tabling, locates people in positions that express the official view of their status in the organisation. Time-tabling is, of course, more than just the determining of time and place of lessons and lecturers. It is concerned with the whole allocation of time to essential activities in the organisation. Secondary schools generally overlook administrative considerations except for allowing time for organisational tasks to certain trained individuals (counselling staff, management team, house heads, etc.). Further and Higher Education also provide a calendar of events around which lectures are organised. On the whole, very little account is taken of the time needed for development activities though in some cases staff are given large blocks of time (even up to a year) to develop courses and programmes. It is in the context of all the other demands made upon staff and their career needs that innovation has to occur. An individual member of staff will be mainly concerned to see that any activity in which he is engaged furthers his professional standing in career terms and/or organisational approval.

There really is little evidence that curriculum change occurs as a consequence of planning though it may follow from what is perceived as a government initiative. The Robbins, Newson and Plowden Reports had a considerable impact on schools and Higher Education and they resulted in the availability of financial resources which could be tapped by colleges etc., with an eye to the main chance. But the actual response originated with the culture of the organisation. The Dip.HE's are a case in point where each reflects the culture (and philosophy?) of the sponsoring institution and even more probably indicates the interests of the head of the institution. It may well be more profitable to examine inter-institutional politics* rather than planning processes in order to understand curriculum change. But however important external factors may be, the critical elements in educational planning have to do with the interpersonal relationships among decision makers; unless we understand how people behave, we can never understand how they use data and technical processes.

---

* *No history of the CNAA will be complete if it does not deal fully with inter-institutional politics.*

13.
Now, What About Adult Education

Adult Education is one of the uncertain areas of education. It is a vague concept that cannot easily be encapsulated as other aspects are in the terms primary, pre-school, secondary and so on. It is usually thought of as a marginal activity and something of an embarrassing addition. Financial cuts in education hit hardest in this area. Even the Russell Report did not effect a clarification of the concept in practical terms and post-Russell implementation has been derisory.

It would appear that Adult Education embraces the following kinds of activities:

.   Non-vocational classes in Further Education (e.g. yoga, flower arranging, handicrafts)
.   Adult Education Colleges and Settlements (e.g. literary studies and local studies)
.   Ruskin and Working Mens Colleges, Northern College (Politics, Trade Union Studies, Literature etc.)
.   University Extension and Adult Education Departments (often rarified and patronising)
.   Management and Industrial Training (generally in special industrially sponsored colleges)
.   Open University
.   Birkbeck College
.   Community Development (an amorphous area of socio-political activism)
.   Basic Education
.   Semi-professional training e.g. Marriage Guidance Counselling

By and large Adult Education falls into the Further Education section of educational provision with some overlap into Higher Education where it is most formalised and traditional. The essential view of Adult Education appears to be that it is some form of "Extension" study and there is an unclear division between vocational and non-vocational courses and programmes, between academic and general interest.

With the rise of the Open University the idea of Higher Education for those who have missed out on formal education became an important feature of educational thinking, the idea of 'distance learning' became associated with it. Elsewhere, particularly in North America more radical approaches developed in such ventures as Antioch College, the California Western University and the Radio College of Ontario. The three strands of development have, therefore, been:

1. Formal and traditional courses leading to awards such as diplomas and degrees of University or similar standing.
2. Formal courses in conventional academic areas but without an award and,

3. innovative courses which try to follow a different study pattern but which lead to a traditionally titled award. (e.g. Ph.D. Antioch).

Higher education is organised almost everywhere on a sequential basis. Higher Education is the final level of attainment after primary, secondary and further education. The term tertiary education is not entirely justified because there is a real distinction made between 'further' and 'higher' education even if the distinction is blurred in particular institutions. Higher Education may be taken to mean 'university degree level of attainment' but Higher Education Institutions tend to ascribe degree and post-degree level to their work just because they provide it (the DMS* is a case in point, post-graduate in time but not in quality). Because an institution of Higher Education is statutorily set up to deal in Higher Education it becomes difficult for it to engage in teaching activity which may be considered of a lower levels, i.e. Further Education. In any case, Further Education Institutions are jealous of their catchment.

So long as Higher Education is thought of as only possible as the last stage of a necessary sequence, there can be little hope of it making a significant contribution to the population at large. On such a premise, Higher Education is highly selective, solely élitist and exclusive for it is only available to those who have considerable academic attainment documented in prescribed and traditional forms (degrees, diplomas). Yet one of the outstanding expectations for the polytechnics was that they should not be élitist in the traditional university sense but would relate much more closely with social needs. To consider that relating to social needs is only possible by giving a practical as opposed to theoretical bias to high academic content in degrees and diplomas is to miss the significance and challenge of the polytechnic concept. There must surely be other ways of relating Higher Education to society at large. For polytechnics this is the issue of adult education and also the crisis of their raison d'etre.

The polytechnics were established specifically to cater for a new form of educational demand, a demand by the adult population at large and not just students in the 18-21 age group. The role of the polytechnics is set out in the government White Paper of 1966 (Cmnd 3006) entitled "A Plan for Polytechnics and Other Colleges". The paper specifically declared:

"Within Higher Education there are two other sets of students no less important than those who have the time and ability to take full-time or sandwich courses of degree standard. The first are those who are seeking a qualification that requires a course of

---

* *Diploma in Management Studies.*

168

higher education which is below degree standard; the second are the many thousands of students who, being already in employment, can find time for only part-time day and/or evening courses, whether they lead to a degree or a qualification below that standard. The Government believe it to be of the utmost importance that the leading colleges concerned with higher education should be comprehensive in the sense that they plan their provision of courses to meet the needs of students in all three categories.

The comprehensive range and character of the work of these centres will broadly distinguish them from other kinds of higher education institutions. As mixed communities of full-time and part-time teachers and students, they will as a whole have closer and more direct links with business, industry and the professions."

Such statements can be variously interpreted and in any case are open ɔ change as needs change, but they indicate an essential concern ⸿hich can be legitimately broadened to raise questions about the mode ⸿ which courses are offered and especially the provision of short ɔurses. The Committee of Polytechnic Directors amplify the position in ⸌eir statement "Many Arts, Many Skills" (1974) where they say:

"Higher Education is no longer a marginal activity affecting very few in the community; it will reach and affect many more in the future. Our task is to be outward looking institutions meeting the educational needs of the majority of those for whom the expansion of Higher Education is required.

Most students will not become professional scholars in the traditional sense; they will leave after their formal education to participate in the work of the community, capable of giving life, reality and substance to theoretical ideas. They will become managers, trade unionists, social workers, professional workers, teachers, designers — practitioners of all kinds. The role of the polytechnics is the professional teaching of the practical arts, the many arts and many skills, at all the levels of scholarship which constitute higher education and are requird by modern professionalism. Over the whole range of academic levels of our work, our aim is to equip our students for active involvement in work and citizenship, so that in their chosen professions they can apply their knowledge, their intellects and their imagination to the complex and intractible situations with which they will be inevitably confronted, and so that, in addition to gaining some measure of mastery and the means for living, they can value the quality of life."

Again, more educational provision than simply traditional courses is ⸌mplied if such a policy is to be put into realistic practice. There is just no way that the conventional qualification programme provides adequat training for the life-long demands of professional and private life.

The problems of Higher Education have continued to exercise th minds of educators since the late nineteen sixties because it has becom increasingly clear that the termination of education somewhe between the ages of 16 and 25 just does not relate to social ar economic needs. Higher Education can no longer be thought of as th topping on Adult education, a terminal point when all is now finishe Many issues of continuing education are unresolved. One of the mo imaginative attempts to examine the problems of 'post-secondar education was made by the government of Ontario Province, Canada, the early nineteen seventies. In the official report, "The Learnir Society", the problem of adult education as distinct from full-tim 'professional' education is faced:

"But if adult education is to realise the new promises of continuing education, it can no longer be treated as a peripheral activity. Some persistent problems will have to be overcome. One is a state of mind, the legacy of a persistent attitude in some colleges and universities that they should be set apart from society: that 'popular education' must be trivial and can grievously harm the primary function of the community of scholars, which are perceived to be the teaching of full-time undergraduates and graduates, research, the perpetuation of intellectual activity, and the maintenance of high academic standards. At only a few centres do adult and part-time students enjoy the status accorded to full-time learners and have programmes specifically tailored to their needs. In other institutions, their low status is constantly reinforced and symbolised by the fact that the teaching of most of their courses is organised on an overload basis, as an extra activity for staff pursuing salary supplements."*

The situation in the United Kingdom is not precisely the same as i Canada but the issues are the same. The general view of Adult Educatio has become trivialised and is still thought of pejoratively as ; 'recreational' activity. Certainly the polytechnics have become anythin but community colleges and where they do have community activitie they are treated as marginal in almost every sense even if the reasons ar understandable. Unquestionably the idea of continuing education – o recurrent education as it has come to be termed – needs much mor consideration. The Ontario Commission continues by discussin necessary development in post-secondary education.

---

* The Learning Society: Report of the Commission on Post-Secondary education i Ontario 1973, Ontario Ministry of Education pp 22–23.

A post-secondary system committed to the individual and aspiring to be accessible, diverse in its functions and programmes, flexible in its modes and standards of learning and evaluation, equitable, and publicly accountable will require departures in five main area. First there must be an expansion of alternatives to formal, institutionalised post-secondary education for those completing their high-school education. Second, colleges, universities and other institutions must enlarge their programmes and means of delivery in the field of education and manpower training, without abandoning their present roles or compromising their integrity. Third, altogether new educational enterprises must be initiated and libraries, museums, art galleries and similar centres must be recognised as important participants in the learning systems. Fourth, the options within post-secondary education must be made readily available. Finally, means must be found to recognise and, where desired, to certify the level and quality of learning acquired in any setting.*

A changed provision in higher education has come to be thought of as recurrent education. A most useful and important symposium on the idea has been edited by Vincent Houghton and Ken Richards of the Open University†. Many important issues of theory and implementation are discussed though the significance of what is required is daunting. The term 'recurrent education' originates in discussions and investigations by the Centre for Educational Research and Innovation (CERI), an OECD agency. In a report published in 1973 it is stated:

"The concept of 'recurrent education' intends to propose a concrete framework within which a great part of the individual's lifelone learning can take place. It differs from the concept of 'permanent education' by making the principles of alteration between education and other activities central to the definition‡".

but this report goes on to say:

"Recurrent education is a proposal for an alternative educational strategy, the guiding principle of which is the fundamental right of the individual to decide his own future. One of the essential characteristics [.....] proceeds from this: it implies getting away from a rigid instructionalised system that imposes its values and objectives upon its students, and developing a framework for

---

* The Learning Society: Report of the Commission on Post-Secondary Education in Ontario, Ontario Ministry of Education 1973 pp. 39.
† Houghton, Vincent & Richards Ken (Eds) *"Recurrent Education: A Plea for Lifelong Learning"* Ward Lock Educational 1974.
‡ *"Recurrent Education: A Strategy for Lifelong Learning"* OECD, Paris 1973 p. 12.

171

participation in decision-making in all aspects of the system, including its objectives and ways and means to achieve them. But taken out of its social and political context, such a participation in decision-making is no more than a smoke screen for a policy precisely the opposite of that which it is said to pursue. The ability to set one's own objectives and to choose between policies is precisely one of the outcomes of a recurrent education strategy aimed at providing full scope for individual development and real equality of educational opportunity . . . Recurrent education is meant to provide a more efficient strategy for achieving essential educational objectives than the traditional system. The chief motivation for recurrent education stems from dissatisfaction with the performance of the present educational system and the conviction that its further straightforward expansion will not improve, and might indeed worsen the situation . . . [The issues are] individual development, equality of opportunity and the interplay between education and society (particularly in connection with the labour market)*.

In the United Kingdom, the Russell Report was an attempt to examine the implications of adult education and while it provided a good summary of the situation did not lead to any really effective change in provision. As with so many government reports, the excitement it generated was more about the report itself than a commitment to action largely because the proposals were typically bureaucratic and unwieldy. Certainly, the Report does not face the issues of cooperation among all agencies concerned in adult education nor the part that the larger traditional institutions (polytechnics, universities, colleges) should play. There is no mention of a fundamental change in the organisation of post-secondary education.

However, the Report does outline the 'needs' of education (the term "permanent education" which is used has now fallen somewhat out of use) and they are worth repeating here:

58.1 We can identify those needs that are related to the functioning of the education service and particularly to the goal of equality of educational opportunity. By this we mean equality of opportunity for each individual actually to benefit, according to his personal capacities, from the total range of educational provision, and not simply to compete for its benefits, which is what equality of opportunity has often meant in practice. To this extent we are in accord with the concept of "permanent education". These needs may be summed up as follows:

---

* "Recurrent Education: A Strategy for Lifelong Learning" OECD, Paris 1973 pp. 32–33.

58.1.1   Remedial education, or the completion of the schools' unfinished tasks. There will be many levels of this, from basic literacy upwards.

58.1.2   Balancing education: that is, filling in the gaps left by the inevitable specialisation of schools and colleges.

58.1.3   Second-chance education, or the opportunity to acquire qualifications whose relevance to the individual has become clear in adult life. The term "second-chance education" has gained currency, but it is not to be interpreted strictly: the needs may equally be for third, fourth or *nth* chances.

58.1.4   Up-dating, or the opportunity to keep abreast of developments in fields where knowledge is rapidly expanding.

58.1.5   Education about education, or the planned promotion of an educative environment, in and around the family home, at work, and elsewhere, which will support and reinforce the work of the schools and colleges and not run counter to it. There can be no true system of education without this.

58.1.6   Counselling and the clarification of choices. There are two related needs here: for information about the range of educational opportunity provided and for help to an individual in assessing his own objectives and capacities in relation to those opportunities.

58.2 Then we can identify those needs that are related to individual personal developments; for example:

58.2.1   Creativity, or the opportunity to fulfil oneself in creative activity of many kinds, ranging from the arts, like painting and three-dimensional arts and crafts, music, drama, dance, speech and writing, to problem-solving, mathematics and scientific activity.

58.2.2   Physical activity, especially the cultivation of skill in recrative pursuits, games and outdoor activities.

58.2.3   Educative social activity, or the opportunity for self-discovery and self-expression in groups of common interest. The health and vitality of local communities may depend as much on the meeting of this need as upon any other single form of activity.

58.2.4   Intellectual activity, towards which all other forms of education are likely to act as a stimulus.

Those who are handicapped, disadvantaged, in hospitals, prisons or otherwise prevented from engaging in the general provision of

173

adult education will, in most cases, have the personal needs identified above and will also have particular needs related to their circumstances, including the need to be helped towards re-integration into general society.

58.3   There are those needs that are related to the place of the individual in society; for example:

58.3.1   "Role education", directed not to training for qualification but to providing the background of knowledge, especially in relation to social change, through which the individual's role can be more responsibly discharged in society, in industry, in voluntary service or in public work of any kind. Here again there will be many forms: examples are education for magistrates or policemen, for clergy or social workers, for shop stewards and trade unionists, for managers and local government officers.

58.3.2   Social and political education of very broad kinds, designed to enable the individual to understand and play his part as citizen, voluntary worker, consumer.

58.3.3   Community education, or providing the background of knowledge and understanding upon which effective action for community purposes, including community development in the strict sense, can be founded.

58.3.4   Education for social leadership. One of the prime needs here is for learning situations in which those with potentialities for leadership (including opinion-leaders) can discover themselves and try themselves out, rather than for set schemes that prepare and train leaders who have been selected in other ways.

It would be difficult to disagree with such an analysis, yet it does not go far enough because the needs are conceived as being capable of gratification in traditional modes within the conventional English system. Further thinking is required of the quality of the Ontario Government Report and those concerned with the amplification of the "recurrent" concept in education. These are still early days for new models of education and we must not be distracted by a current increase in what are on closer analysis 'traditional' forms cosmetically represented — for instance, the Northern College — or even second chance schemes like the 'Open College' at Nelson and Colne.

Somehow we need to be able to rethink completely what we mean by education itself let alone 'Adult' education. Some of the most creative thinking about education and the way it is organised has come from those who have considered educational organisation in the third world and low-income countries. The traditional pattern and conception of education has been neatly summarised by Ian Lister in a paper, *Criteria for Alternatives in Education, with Special Reference to low-income countries**. He describes the stereotype of traditional education with the dominance of the teacher and the political consequences of systems which have professional teachers, the stereotyping of school knowledge as arcane, the false sequencing of school knowledge with the consequence of screening and selecting, and the organising of the school system to retain hierarchical control over students. Conventionally organised education is little more than a political weapon if it is used only as a means of channelling power in favour of an already established elite.

Firstly, if we are to be able seriously to rethink the nature of adult education — where we have potentially more freedom from traditional patterns than anywhere else in education — we need to seek alternatives to the traditional concept. To begin with, we may consider learning to be a partnership rather than a hierarchy. In such a situation, teachers and students are partners in learning; both are learners and both are teachers. This is a radical difference in relationship from that which currently exists (even among teachers themselves). There is no reason to assume that adult students are less experienced or even less qualified on the whole learning process than teachers. A learning process involves much more than simply content, or cognition, it involves the whole affective situation and relationship. The student knows a great deal more about himself, how he learns and how he is progressing than the teacher. The teacher's assumptions about axioms and linearity in a subject area may be quite wrong. Only in subjects like mathematics — and only then 'perhaps' — does the artificial logic of the subject predetermine the linearity of learning.

Secondly, we need to re-examine the forms of learning in terms of location and lesson structure. The hour to one-and-a-half hour lecture is an administrative construction that has nothing whatsoever to do with either learning or teaching. There are many other structural forms for learning and especially adult learning. Learning is a complex psychological process which involves more than application to a simple abstract factual problem or issue. Each step in learning is a complex of personal concerns; the traditional 'class' has little value in the complexity of learning for young people let alone adults. It is not unimportant to recall that in adult education general social activity

---

* Ian Lister, Department of Education, University of York 1975 (mimeographed).

dominates the learning situation and residence is a highly valuable aspect of adult education courses. Residence permits the creation and development of a learning ambience that separates one activity (ordinary life) from the other (the specific learning situation).

Thirdly, we need to change our view of education as being simply additive, that is the adding on of new learning to old. We can think of education as being a 'filling out', an enrichment of what is already there so that as we learn more there is a total change within the individual, a qualitative change throughout the personality. We can then be in a position to view Higher Education (and not only Higher but all other forms) as a somewhat different process from the generally familiar one. If we view Higher Education as enrichment then it is not a third or fourth level that must await its time in a sequence of events but is rather a quality of educational (or learning) experience that can happen virtually at any time (and in any way) in an individual's life history.

For example, none of us progresses to a Higher level on all aspects of our learning or cognition. A genius in music will be more skilled at five or six years than most adults will ever be. An artisan (if there are still such people) with little formal education can be a world expert in an area of his enthusiasm, say, pigeon breeding. After all, a member of the English nobility who has been educated privately at home, can hob-nob on equality with Oxbridge Dons because he has the social and linguistic background so to do, not by virtue of having a chain of degrees. The purpose of Higher Education is not soley linear addition but continual enrichment.

To bring about such a change we need to alter almost completely our mode of teaching. We need to think of collaborative learning rather than didactic. To do this we shall need to develop new ways of helping in the learning process in all probability based on an affective grounding. Forms of experiential learning are involved here where attitudes and values are the first concern, and learners join together in a mutual exploration. We have some experience of such modes in the Dip.HE, sensitivity training, creative workshops, team research and collaborative projects in Staff Development. In all likelihood we have only begun to touch the tip of the possibilities.

The time is ripe for a new start in the institutions of higher education. We should engage in two related thrusts. One is to explore and develop new ways of learning/teaching with conventional groups (e.g. new programmes in Staff Development) and new groups (e.g. trade union leaders). This would be a form of action research. The other thrust would be to implement a programme in teacher training in adult education. This would fall in the conventional brief of almost every Institute of Higher Education with a responsibility for teacher training but it would also enable us to practice our precepts and facilitate an early involvement in the newer ideas of Adult Education. We would also need to experiment with new locations and structures for education and training and should not feel constrained by our own conventional patterns. We should make submissions for a national Diploma in the Education of Adults as a practical model and test of our theoretical position (for example, the submission would raise issues of entrance qualifications, standard of attainment, measurement and evaluations, accreditation, acceptability with a profession or outside bodies. It would be alive model). At the same time, each institution needs to examine the traditional view of, and approaches to, Adult Education to see if what gaps there are in the conventional provision.

Unless the Institutions of Higher Education take an initiative, the whole educational edifice will come crumbling down as it becomes increasingly remote from social needs and economic reality. Paradoxically, the point of change is with the cinderella of the educational system, Adult Education.

AN INITIAL BIBLIOGRAPHY FOR ADULT EDUCATION

CERI, *Recurrent Education: A Strategy for Lifelong Learning* Paris, OECD, 1973.

A Choice of Futures, Report of the Commission on Educational Planning, Alberta (Worth Report) 1972.

Council of Europe: *Case Studies in Permanent Education* Strasbourg 1967.

Houghton, Vincent & Richards, Ken (Eds): *Recurrent Education: A Plea for Lifelong Learning:* Ward Lock Educational 1974.

Houghton, Vincent, *Recurrent Education: An Alternative Failing* Open University (Unit 16 Couse E221) 1974.

Huberman, Michael: *Reflections on Democratisation of Secondary and Higher Education:* UNESCO 1970.

Hutchins, Robert M: *The Learning Society:* Penguin 1968.

Husen, Torsten: The Learning Society, Methuen 1974.

The Learning Society: Report of the Commission on Post Secondary Education, Ontario 1973 (The Wright Report).

Lister, Ian: *Criteria for alternatives in Education with special reference to low-income countries:* Department of Education, University of York, (mimeographed) 1975.

Lister, Ian: *Alternatives in Higher Education,* Department of Education, University of York, (mimeographed) 1975.

The Russell Report: HMSO 1975.

Many Arts, Many Skills: Committee of Directors of Polytechnics 1974.